How to Resolve Conflicts at Work

How to Resolve Conflicts at Work

A Take-Charge Assistant Book

Florence M. Stone

AMACOM
American Management Association

New York • Atlanta • Boston • Chicago • Kansas City • San Francisco • Washington, D.C.
Brussels • Mexico City • Tokyo • Toronto

This publication is designed to provide accurate and authoritative information in regard to the subject matter covered. It is sold with the understanding that the publisher is not engaged in rendering legal, accounting, or other professional service. If legal advice or other expert assistance is required, the services of a competent professional person should be sought.

Library of Congress Cataloging-in-Publication Data

Stone, Florence M.
    How to resolve conflicts at work : a take-charge assistant book/
    Florence M. Stone
        p.   cm.
    Includes index.
    ISBN 0-8144-7989-8
    1. Conflict management.   I. Title.
    HD42.S76   1999
    658.4'053—dc21   99-26325
                                                                         CIP

Printing number

10 9 8 7 6 5 4 3 2 1

Contents

Dedicated to my sister,
Elsie Marion Stone

How to Resolve Conflicts at Work

Preface: What's In It for Me?

Being an office professional isn't what it once was. Today, as an administrative employee, you have many more responsibilities than your predecessors had. What many of these responsibilities have in common is that they call for you to work with many more people than you did in the past. You now work directly not only with your own boss, her employees, and your own counterparts in other departments within your organization, but act as liaison between your boss and other managers and executives inside your organization. Among those outside your organization with whom you work directly are vendors, suppliers, and customers or representatives of client firms.

Increasingly, too, you are participating in team meetings not only with individuals from your own department but also persons at various levels in your organization in cross-functional teams.

Whether you are acting as your boss's representative or for yourself, as the number of times you interact with others within and outside your organization grows, so, too, does the possibility of your encountering obstacles to doing your work in the form of differences of opinion or difficult persons. If these situations aren't handled well, they can generate into conflicts, and these conflicts, if left unresolved, can so seriously erode relationships that not only your own work but that of your boss, department, or company may be impeded.

If that sounds serious, frankly it is. What begins as a tiff can grow to angry words and hard feelings that never go away and over time can fester and make the workplace unpleasant not only for the original combatants but innocent bystanders as well. However, like many of your other new responsibilities, you can learn the skills you need to prevent your own interactions with others from evolving into conflicts, smooth over sensitive feelings, rebuild relationships with individuals with whom you have had words in the past, and even help others resolve their conflicts by acting as a mediator.

These skills are important to you not only because of the problems they can prevent—anger that saps productivity and draws one's attention to a perceived injustice, the perpetrator, and the desire to get even, rather than to one's work—but because conflict resolution skills are of high value in today's workplace. And, yes, positive work relationships can make your work more satisfying and pleasant and much less stressful.

These are the "WIIFMs" for you to purchase and read this book and develop your conflict management skills. "WIIFM" stands for "What's in it for me?", and, given the time constraints we all have and numerous books out there from which to choose, I believe any author of a business book needs to address this issue up front with a potential reader.

The "C" Words

Among business buzzwords, two of the most popular are "collaboration" and "cooperation." Organizations have found that collaborative, cooperative workforces are the most productive. If you can't resolve disagreements before they escalate into conflicts—whether they are with customers or managers or only other colleagues—you can expect this skill deficiency to influence your career options. Needless to say, if you are unable to talk out a problem without becoming emotional, shouting or otherwise showing your anger, thereby fueling a disagreement, then you can expect more serious repercussions as organizations move more and more toward a collaborative workforce.

Not only do organizations expect their managers to work cooperatively with others and, when differences arise, to resolve conflicts before they impact operations, they expect such behavior of all of their employees.

If you have a reputation for being hot-tempered, getting into loud and angry disagreements, or otherwise being difficult to work with, you're likely to lose points with your boss, no matter how hard you work.

On the other hand, given the importance in which management places on a collaborative, cooperative workplace, you can earn recognition if your boss and others in management see that you work cooperatively with colleagues and even help your colleagues work collaboratively by volunteering to help them resolve their conflicts.

If you supervise others, your role is to take steps to ensure that your employees work well together getting the work done. Supervisors who allow their employees' behavior to threaten departmental productivity, corporate partnerships, or external alliances, aren't likely to remain supervisors for long—maybe not even remain with an organization for long. In my book *The High-Value Manager,* I identified skills, abilities, knowledge, and attitudes critical in the workplace. Conflict resolution skills were among those identified by me and my co-author, Randi T. Sachs, as critical in today's leaner organizations, now and into the future, as functional silos continue to fall, teams become the means by which more work is done, and positional authority becomes increasingly less important.

You may know of managers, even senior executives, who are defensive, ready to argue with anyone who questions their vision or ideas or otherwise disagrees—maybe even your own boss is like this. Let me say that such individuals are in for a rude awakening. You can be sure that these organizational tigers will have to change their stripes and learn a new, more collegial way of managing, if they haven't already started to do so.

What's Wrong with Conflict Anyway?

There is nothing wrong with conflicts *up to a point.* Conflicts can be productive and can even motivate people to excel. Conflict can generate constructive dialogue, from which new ideas are developed, refined, and ultimately successfully implemented.

But conflict can be counterproductive if it results in problems rather than solutions to them. Specific problems that can arise include the following:

- **Conflict can add to the tension in a workplace that is already stressful.** This added tension can mean high absenteeism and tardiness (after all, who wants to work in a stressful work environment?). Besides, the stress within a conflictive workplace can have physical and emotional effects on those within the workplace, from sleepless nights to back pains to heart palpitations and high blood pressure. In other words, conflict in the workplace can make work seem like "work."

- **Conflict can mean poor decisions.** If not properly managed, conflict can make someone blind to facts or deaf to a logical argument. People's good sense can be shelved because the conflict—either due to a desire to prove themselves right or a dislike of the other individuals in a disagreement—prompts them to look for "facts" to prove their preconceived point.

  Sometimes friction between individuals can mean that no decision is made at all—or that information that could help make a good decision is hidden from the decision maker because of a small tiff that has begun to fester.

- **Conflict can mean decisions, good or bad, don't get implemented.** The worth of an idea is not in the idea itself but in its implementation. Ideas, whether right or wrong, are worthless if they aren't implemented. Decisions that are made by one person or group but lack the support of those who are responsible for implementing them just don't get implemented or don't get implemented correctly. Those on the other side of the disagreement choose to drag their feet or don't walk the talk at all.

- **Conflict can mean confusion and ambiguity.** Ever wonder what a ping pong ball feels like? Elaine, an office professional, discovered the feeling when she found herself working for two university professors who decided to collaborate on a research paper. Although they had worked well as colleagues in the English department, they had never worked together on a project. And, as it turned out, they had different methods of approaching research. Elaine found herself doing and then redoing work because, caught between two clashing viewpoints about how to do the task, she tried to accommodate both of her bosses. Even before their differences had reached the shouting stage, Elaine's productivity had severely declined. The situation influenced not only her work on the project but work in general as her frustration took control.

- **Conflict can generate a "get-even" attitude.** Even if one side wins, and their decisions are implemented, the other, losing side may harbor ill feelings and wait out their time to retaliate, for instance when the other side needs a helping hand. Individuals who usually are generous with their time or skills may refuse to assist a co-worker, even if their help would be for the good of the department or organization as a whole, either due to a personality conflict or other dispute or disagreement, even though that disagreement occurred months before. So long as the dispute is still festering—the disagreement has not been resolved in a manner satisfactorily to both parties—the hard feelings continue.

- **Conflict can destroy professional relationships.** Within a department, co-workers choose sides either in a personality conflict or a dispute over an issue; a conflict can thus fractionalize the organization. This, in turn, can influence communication and work within the group as a whole. Loyalty to a friend or a cause can distract employees from the work that needs to be done.

Let's Look at This Book

This book is very different from other books you might find on conflict resolution. It is written specifically for office professionals, and the advice is the kind that you can implement without positional authority. As you read the various stories in its pages, you will find yourself recalling similar situations you either observed or participated in.

The book itself is divided into three sections.

In the first section, you will gain a better understanding of the source of conflicts, and you will also learn how to prevent unnecessary conflicts—without either losing the other party's respect or giving up your chance of being heard out—by practicing controlled disagreement. Admittedly, you can't prevent all differences of opinion from escalating to conflict. So Section I also points out five ways to resolve any conflict you encounter in your work, again without wimping out.

Finally, in this section, you will learn when to blow off steam and when to stay with your emotions—in other words, how to *effectively* use anger to get your way.

Section II of the book examines the three kinds of problems that can generate conflicts—poor communications, personality conflicts, and operating problems—and how to address each.

Finally, in Section III, the book looks at the techniques you can use to build better relationships with those with whom you work—your boss(es), your co-workers and colleagues, and customers and vendors. Since you will be participating more and more in teams, even leading them, the book also includes a chapter on your role as leader or participant in defusing conflicts in a team environment (yes, you don't have to be heading up a team to create a cooperative team environment).

If you still think this isn't an issue of concern to you, take a look at the following ten scenarios. Some reflect productive conflicts, the others are of the kind that managers are anxious to put an end to. Which do you think are which?

Cases in Point

1. Marge and Jean have been asked to work together on a project. Marge believes that "there should be a place for everything and everything should be in its place"; Jean doesn't. And she has said as much to Marge. Marge's co-worker has just spent the last 30 minutes searching for a copy of an article that she needs to reference in a bibliography she's completing. She found it under a stack of papers on Jean's desk. Should Marge tell Jean off for her disorganization or should she just take the article and go back to work?
2. Bryan and Alix disagree with Theresse, who is leader of a team of office professionals formed to look into ways that the department's intranet can be utilized to streamline operations. The two disagree with Theresse's authoritative stance on several issues. Should they say nothing, and allow decisions with which they disagree to be implemented, or should they speak up?
3. Mario works for John. John gave Mario the responsibility for putting together a procedural manual for all the offices under John's authority. Because John will be talking to the head of the San Francisco office, and its head, Tom, has yet to submit his contribution to the manual, John has asked Mario to sit in. During the conference call, in which Tom is connected via phone to Mario

and John in John's office, John repeatedly signals with his hand for Mario to be quiet when Mario starts to speak. Mario believed that he had been asked to participate in the discussion, not solely be a listener. There were several times when Mario felt he could make a positive contribution but each time he was silenced. He's angry and upset. Should he say something to John?

4. Erin is a no-nonsense person who believes that when she has something to say, she should say it—regardless of how it makes others feel. Antonia was promoted over Erin as assistant to the department head. She has a long to-do list, sees that Erin isn't busy, and asks her to lend a hand. Erin refuses, telling Antonia, "You wanted the job; now you've got it." Upset already by the heavy workload, Antonia loses her self-control and rushes to the lady's room where she can have a good cry. You are friends with Antonia and believe that she deserved the promotion. What should you do?

5. Antonia's friend Gloria left the company about a month before. When Gloria visited the office, Antonia put together a lunch with Gloria and her old friends. All were invited except Erin. You thought that Antonia and Erin were getting along well lately, but now you aren't so sure. Some at the lunch think Antonia had the right to invite anyone she wanted; others feel that Erin had a right to be included—she knew Gloria long before Antonia. You assist the head of the division. As the group of office professionals takes sides, you see that divisional work isn't getting done. What should you do, if anything?

6. Tim's assistant is on vacation. During her absence, you have been asked to lend a hand in sales, as well as do your own work. Your work includes covering both Tim's and his assistant's calls. You aren't familiar with all the accounts the company services, so when a salesman calls you aren't able to provide him with the information he wants. You explain that you are substituting for Lynn but you offer to get back to him later in the day with the information. You plan to ask Tim for the information. But Tim is in a meeting all day. You get sidetracked with your own boss's work, and the salesman never hears from you. The next day he calls Tim, who calls you in to tell you that the firm lost an account because of your failure to support the sales operation. You are seething.

How do you handle your discussion with Tim? What do you say to the salesman who calls later in the day demanding new information immediately?

7. Blair is an old friend from your hometown. She now lives in your city and she calls to tell you, surprise, she now works in another department in your company. You offer to show your old pal the ropes, and Monday you begin doing so. You invite Blair to lunch with you and your friends, and you are like Johnny-on-the-spot if Blair has a problem. As the days go by, you notice that a fellow assistant, Marietta, seems annoyed with you, but you don't know why. When she brings some folders to you, and dumps them on your desk scattering other papers there, you ask her what's bothering her. She doesn't mince words: "You sure don't treat Anglos like you treat Hispanics. I had to find my way on my own but all you have to be is white and Anglo-Saxon, and everyone is there for you." What do you say to Marietta?

8. Bill promised Kristin that he would hire a temp to help her with the details of the client meeting he had to hold in Vegas in the spring. When Kristin was told she would be coming with him to take notes and otherwise assist, she offered to put in long hours and weekends in preparing for the meeting, as well as doing her day-to-day work, if he would hold off hiring a temp until they were in Vegas. The temp would free her to spend some time sightseeing—all her life, she said, she had wanted to visit Las Vegas. Kristin was exhausted from the extra workload by the time they arrived in Vegas but she was also excited about her first trip to Vegas—until Bill told her that he had no plans to have a temp there. "You've done such a great job, and you know so much about the conference," he said, "I really would prefer to have you with me." If you were Kristin, what would you say or do?

9. You are heading up a team meeting of the office professionals within your department. Your boss, who heads the department, sees your role as coordinator and he believes these meetings can ensure better clerical support. The rest of the team seems to welcome the meeting sessions—except Margaret. Each time a topic arises, following a very brief discussion, she calls for a vote. Margaret is highly regarded by the rest of the team, and also very out-

spoken, so when you have tried to encourage further discussion, she has silenced objections. On one occasion she accused you of "wasting time better spent doing our jobs." What should you say to Margaret?

10. You are having computer problems. You call Systems and you are told that Todd will be down. You look at Barbara, another office professional, and you can tell she is thinking the same as you. Todd is notorious about promising to come then never showing up until you've made several calls. When he arrives, he throws a variety of technical terms at the user, hints that the person is technologically challenged, then asks the individual to leave as he fixes the machine. He claims having another person in the office distracts him. Once he is done, he never explains what was wrong because, he usually says, "you wouldn't understand." You find his treatment offensive. Should you tolerate it, or risk a conflict by speaking out? If you speak out, what should you say?

These are real-world situations submitted by readers of AMA's newsletter, *The Take-Charge Assistant*. To handle them successfully, you need to draw on the conflict resolution and interpersonal skills described herein. This is a wonderful opportunity for you to grow new skills important in the more collaborative workplaces we are moving toward.

Intuitively, you may already know both your strengths and your weaknesses in this area. But this book offers you an opportunity to overcome shortcomings and refine your skills. Most important, you may find in these pages solutions to problems that you may be having with your boss, even problems you were not aware of before, thereby smoothing your work relationship with him or her. You will learn how to make the most of work relationships with peers and others within your organization by addressing any festering conflicts in an assertive and not a confrontational manner. You will learn how to handle difficult people, both within and outside your organization, with whom you must interact successfully. Not only will you be able to get your job done well and advance in your career, but you will find that your job is less stressful by mastering the interpersonal skills for conflict resolution.

You may even discover in these pages the skills you need to make your interactions with others, which are part of your changing job, fun.

Section I

Overview

1

How Do You Handle Conflict?

Conflict is part of the human condition. And as many things in life, there is a positive as well as a negative side to it. Positive conflict can stimulate increased productivity and improved decision making. It can generate new ways of looking at situations and, consequently, greater creativity. But conflict, unchecked, can create barriers to individual and organizational effectiveness, derailing teamwork and adding to the stress in the workplace.

Nowhere are conflicts more likely to be found than in today's work environments where stress, lean staffing, and job insecurity make it much easier for them to develop. As companies have restructured, employees are expected to work longer hours with fewer resources and are more prone to burnout. This creates an environment primed for differences in values, beliefs, and viewpoints, and miscommunications that lead to arguments and conflicts. Conflicts can arise over small matters that are easily resolved and soon forgotten, but they can also arise and then escalate to the point where the hostile emotions affect the job performance of the parties involved or that of spectators who either are distracted or take sides in the issue.

No question, at one time or another, all of us have probably been an observer, if not a participant, in a disagreement with one or more co-workers, our boss or another manager, or one or more customers or vendors. Sometimes the conflict takes the form of a look (you know the kind I mean). Sometimes the conflict is spoken, with the tone and amplitude of the words exchanged a reflection of the emotions felt. Sometimes conflict can become physical, with one or both parties becoming annoyed enough with the other to want to throw a punch. The worst-case scenario is when conflict takes the form of violent behavior by one person against another or many others with whom the person works.

Conflicts arise from various situations—from something as trivial within a group as when or where to hold meetings, to the question of who within the group should get new computers and who will have to be happy with only upgrades, to major departmental issues such as who will report to whom, how to reorganize the staff, even the issue of whether the department should continue to exist.

Today's lean organizations have staff with too much to do and too little time to do it, which is enough to generate angry words, but add the scarce resources in many organizations, the diverse backgrounds and personalities of those within these organizations, and their different ideas about what needs to be done and how they should be done, and you have an explosive mixture.

One Big Happy Family?

During corporate meetings, top executives often will brag about how "the company is one big happy family, without conflicts or problems." I have yet to meet any member of such a fortunate family circle. Certainly, based on my own work experience and interactions with managers from myriad organizations, I find it hard to believe that there is truly an organization out there where there are no conflicts.

This is true despite the current focus within organizations on teams and teamwork. In fact, there may be more reason for conflict as companies promote concepts related to collaboration and cooperation at the same time that they recognize and reward those with reputations as tough street fighters who are willing to win at all costs.

It doesn't matter what the organization's size. All organizations are made up of groups of individuals. Within the groups, the needs, values, goals, and means of working of individual members may be very different. Among the groups—whether as diverse as marketing and production, or two production groups—different self-interests may pull them in different directions.

The Sources of Conflict

Conflicts don't arise without cause, and they usually don't disappear until the cause is addressed. If a conflict isn't resolved, or at least its effects tempered, the conflict's effects can grow.

In today's team-based organizations, conflicts that end up costing the organization money—from poor cooperation or collaboration to lost innovations and declining productivity—can also hurt the careers of those who are parties to a conflict but who do nothing to build fences.

Most conflicts are founded in resource limitations, psychological needs, or value differences. Conflicts over limited resources, such as supplies or latest technology, are among the easiest to manage. The need to be liked and respected causes conflict when an employer promotes one person over another, or when one individual is excluded from meetings that her peers are invited to attend. The majority of conflicts stem from value differences and are the most difficult to resolve.

Conflicts also arise from differences in viewpoints. You may believe in reorganizing office procedures, whereas a colleague wants to keep things just as they are. Another co-worker may want to keep copies of the magazines her boss receives in her work station where they are easily accessible, whereas you may want to put together a department library in which all periodicals are stored together and accessible to everyone in the organization. In each instance, a conflict can arise. Just as there are never enough resources within your company or department to satisfy everyone's needs, so there never can be unanimity on every point.

Competition or rivalry between individuals or even groups can also cause conflicts. Disputes are likely to arise between two people who must work together when both are in line for promotion. Two teams within an organization may trip over each other as they both compete to head up a high-visibility project. The rivalry is based not only on access to the resources to do the work but also on the prestige that will come from the team that gets the leading role in the project.

Some conflicts arise because lines of authority aren't clearly delineated. This is particularly a problem today as companies espouse empowerment yet many managers provide only lip service to the concept. You want to make decisions and implement ideas in areas outside your job responsibility, whereas your boss sees your responsibility limited to the boundaries of your job description or, worse, to her orders. You may have been with your organization long enough to tell a junior manager how to do things, but this staff member may resent your intrusion into his job and even see your help as threatening. One team may implement changes in office procedures without first checking in advance with staff members and others who are affected by the change. Any time individuals or groups feel that their authority has been usurped or that their authority is being questioned, conflicts can arise.

Then there are those instances when conflicts arise just because people can't get along well. Someone may be aggressive and generate an aggressive response in kind. Another person may be insecure or still another person may be defensive. Whatever the cause, the people clash. In some instances, there are no other reasons for the problem than that the two people just don't like each other.

So you can have conflicts between two individuals (interpersonal), between one person and a group (intrapersonal), and between two formal or informal groups (intergroup).

No question, the most uncomfortable conflicts are those you might have between you and your boss or some individual in a higher position than you. In resolving such a conflict, the difficulty is in overcoming the intimidation and sense of forced compliance that the person's position seems to grant him. Even in such circumstances, however, you should attempt to resolve the conflict. You should feel free to air your complaints in a constructive manner—without fear of repercusion. You should have the opportunity to state your case without interruption, be given a clear picture of management's position on the matter, and be given the opportunity to work with your boss in finding a solution to the problem.

Approaches to Conflict

How we respond to conflicts is determined by our personalities, which are a reflection of our nurturing as children, the importance of the issue to us, and the weight we place on maintaining a good working relationship with another or others in our organization. When faced with a conflict, researchers have found that people respond in one of these ways: ignore the situation; get aggressive; make love, not war; seek the middle ground; or take an ideal conflict resolution approach.

Ignoring the Situation

Like ostriches, some of us bury our heads in the sand, avoiding both the issue and those with whom we are in disagreement. We doubt we can win so we don't confront the issue despite the impact that the problem might have on our ability to do our work.

Clearly, ignoring a conflict may only make it worse; it doesn't guarantee that the problem will disappear. Further, it's an approach to conflicting situations that can't be used too often. Otherwise, in time, as you withdraw from one conflict and another, rather than attempt to resolve them, you get the reputation as a wimp, and others perceive you as someone they can walk over. Management isn't blind, either. You are unlikely to be considered for advancement, certainly not into a management position. When a manager acts like an ostrich when faced with a conflict, she loses the respect of those whose work she oversees.

Getting Aggressive

Janine, assistant to the head of marketing, preferred to "look the other way" when problems arose between her and members of the marketing staff. Consequently, her appointment as team leader to a group of staff members, with the mission of streamlining the department's work with several ad agencies, was a fiasco from the first meeting. Team members either refused assignments on the basis of too much work already, or agreed grudgingly to do their tasks, then turned in less-than-perfect work if anything at all. As the group found they could pretty much get away with anything with Janine, attendance at the meetings dropped until, finally, Janine found herself with e-mail excuses from each and every member about why they couldn't attend the session that afternoon.

As Janine sat alone in the department meeting room, she knew what had prompted this behavior by the team members: She had had the *audacity,* in their opinion, to make suggestions at a staff meeting in which she was a participant and, indeed, to question the need for so much paperwork between the department and ad firms they used. This meant questioning some of the procedures imposed earlier by Mike, one of the most creative but also most temperamental members of the staff. It was Janine's recommendations that had prompted her leadership role on the team—but they were also the reason for her poor treatment by the department's staff.

Janine knew that she had to remedy the problem. She wanted to move into marketing herself, which meant that the team had to accomplish its mission on schedule. She couldn't do it as things stood now, so she decided that her only other alternative was to get tough with team members even if in the longer term it meant a worse relationship with the staff.

In choosing to force the issue, Janine took a popular approach to resolving conflicts. Many people see resolution as a matter of win-lose, and they want to win, often because it makes them feel powerful over the other person. Losing makes them feel like a failure. Janine wasn't interested in increasing her power base; rather, she felt that the team effort would fail if she didn't take charge.

The aggressive style involves threats and ultimatums, which Janine used, calling each of the team members to let them know that if they didn't cooperate with her she would report it to their mutual boss.

Needless to say, an aggressive response to conflicts infrequently wins points with spectators, much less participants, in the conflict. Many firms consider aggressive behavior as grounds for termination. Some firms recommend that employees who practice an aggressive style participate in the organization's employee assistance program for counseling to help them with interpersonal conflicts on the job.

And with cause. Rarely does such behavior resolve a conflict although it might seem to do so over the short term. Over the longer term, however, it only adds further cause for anger. Which is what happened to Janine. The team's members did mend their ways and ultimately supported the group's mission. The assignment was completed on schedule, and to the satisfaction of the head of marketing. But over the longer term, Janine found herself on the outs with almost all the department's members.

Opportunities to learn by working with marketing staff were closed to her unless she went to her boss to get him to ask the staff member to train her. Unfortunately, as her boss demanded more and more of her time to work on administrative details and to provide clerical support, he became less inclined to give her these opportunities.

In the end, the ostrich-turned-lion had to leave the organization to find the kind of department and colleagues who would give her an opportunity to increase her employability and ultimately to take on a marketing role and eventually a managerial role.

Did the experience teach Janine anything? Yes, ostriches don't get ahead, and lions or lionesses eventually trap themselves.

Make Love, Not War

There are individuals so concerned about their relationship with the other party that they won't discuss the conflict for fear that the discussion might damage their relationship. They'd rather give up job satisfaction and comfort than take the risk of confronting the issue and seeking some kind of resolution of the problem between them and the other person. Take Pamela. She's a very different person in work than when she is at home. At home, she is very open with her family. If there is a problem, she will talk it out with her husband or daughter Sandra. On the other hand, in the office Pamela is a timid mouse, allowing herself to be put upon by co-workers and her abusive boss without a squeak. Several years ago, Pam was laid off from her job almost immediately after making a formal complaint about her work situation. Whether there was or there wasn't a relationship between the two events, Pamela believes there was. She shies away from confrontations for fear of a repetition of that situation. She and her husband both need to work to put aside enough money to pay for their daughter's education, and Pamela has no intention of jeopardizing her job by speaking up even if she is in the right.

Those who walk away from conflict soon find themselves walked over. Others know that they can take advantage of them, and they do so, consciously or unconsciously.

Seekers of a Middle Ground

These individuals are as concrned with their own needs as they are with their relationship with the other party. So they seek a middle ground, although it may mean that they have to sacrifice most, if not all, of their goals to restore their good relationship with the person with whom they are having a conflict.

We're not talking compromise here since these individuals still value the relationship more than their own needs.

Ultimately, we come to the best solution.

Look on the Situation as a Problem

These individuals want a workable answer that will satisfy both their own and the other person's needs. They believe that the relationship will be retained if both they and the other party are satisfied from the negotiations. They want a mutually satisfactory solution to the conflict, which they see as a problem rather than confrontation.

This is the ideal approach to conflict resolution in that it should lead to a solution that represents the best interests of all in the conflict, including the organization. The parties to the conflict develop into partners; they no longer are adversaries. The seeds of future conflicts are removed, and there is nothing left to fester.

The problem solving process is a six-step process. We describe this process in greater detail in Section II of the book. But the process involves doing the following:

- **Define the needs of each party to the conflit.** This step recognizes the fact that each individual brings to the conflict a different perspective. For collaboration to take place, time needs to be spent in understanding all views about the situation.

- **Generate as many solutions as possible.** The conflict can be handled in various ways. As part of the six-step process, you need to identify as many alternatives as possible.
- **Identify the best among good ideas for resolving the problem.** You're looking for the solution that fulfills the needs of both parties to the conflict.
- **Make it so.** Once you've chosen the best solution in conjunction with the other party, you need to plan how the solution will be implemented.
- **Implement the plan.** The conflict won't be resolved unless the plan is fully implemented. That means input from both parties during this stage of the process.
- **Monitor the result.** You want to be sure the process is working and that new conflicts aren't developing.

One caveat to this process: It won't work if emotions continue to run high. Which is why the process should not begin until you and the other party have met and you've given the individual the opportunity to vent her feelings. When feelings run high, they need to be addressed, or the conflict will only be buried.

How Do You Rate?

Which approach to conflict management do you usually take when faced with differences that are turning into a conflict?

- Are problems that concern you handled by others?
- Are your ideas and comments ignored?
- Do you feel your concerns aren't being met?

If you say "yes" to these three questions, it could mean that you often wimp out when faced with conflicts.

- Is negotiating different for you?
- Do you find it hard to make concessions to others?
- Are you unable to say, "I'm sorry"?

If you say "yes" to these, you may be more inclined to fight than compromise.

- Do others get their way while you don't?
- Do you listen to others' issues but keep your own needs to yourself?
- Do you see being conciliatory as important?

If you say "yes" to these, you prefer to maintain your relationships with those with whom you are in conflict rather than understand the source of a conflict and resolve it.

- Do you go for what will work rather than what's needed?
- Do you find it hard to push for what you need?
- Do problems with people recur?

If you say "yes" to these, you are a middle grounder, seeking compromise. Often when the compromise doesn't work, the conflict returns.

- Do you dig for the reasons behind the problem?
- Do you ask questions to better understand the other person's feelings?
- Do you set action steps to avoid a recurrence of a conflict situation?

If you say "yes" to these final three questions, you tend to seek out solutions to conflicts and resolve them by getting to their cause. This is your favored approach.

One Key Point

While problem solving is the most effective and efficient approach to conflict resolution, the other four have their place. For instance, you might withdraw from a conflict if you thought you couldn't win or needed more time to prepare to discuss an issue. Sometimes, too, addressing the conflict may not be worth the time it takes or there is truly the likelihood that the problem will disappear.

Taking an aggressive stance might make sense if the stakes are very high or the issue very important to you, or the need to have a good relationship is less important than your being right. In the case of "make love, not war," on the other hand, the relationship is more important than the goal. Stakes are low and consequently worth giving up to maintain harmony with the other person. Or this tactic might make sense if you expect to lose all if you enter into negotiation or problem solving.

Negotiation's purpose is to reach compromise, and it's the best tactic when you're not sure you are right or when there is the possibility of your losing because the other person either is in a superior position or has others in power on their side. It also sends a message to others that you don't want to fight over the issue but rather reach a win-win solution.

Unfortunately, in compromise one person invariably wins more than the other, which can lead to a new cause of conflict.

The problem solving approach, if it truly achieves collaboration, will salvage the relationship at the same time that it achieves the best solution. Keep in mind that the best solution may not favor you more than the other person, but rather will create a foundation for a better relationship in the future. It's this last reason that it should be most frequently practiced if time and other factors allow.

In the next chapter, you will look at those emotional needs within yourself that influence your response to a conflict—in particular, whether you allow a difference to develop into a conflict.

2

Keeping Emotions Under Control

Resolving a conflict by determining its cause may be the best way to end a difference that has already reached confrontation stage. But better yet is to prevent a conflict from reaching that confrontation stage at all. Ideally, you should take action before angry words are exchanged and the likelihood of a collaborative, cooperative relationship is thereby limited. As I say elsewhere in this book, it's hard to take back words said in heat; they leave an indelible impression not only on the person to whom they were directed but also on the speaker.

Since conflicts involve two or more people, any discussion of clash control has to recognize that we all have hot buttons that can trigger emotional reactions—even you have these buttons. For clash control, you need to know, first, those issues or comments that may stimulate an intense emotional reaction on your part. Once you have control of your own hot buttons, you are better able to address rationally any difference that arises.

To identify your emotional triggers, here are some questions to ask yourself:

- What accomplishment am I most proud of? Would others agree?
- What do others see as my weaknesses? Do I agree?
- What individual or situation do I try to avoid during my day and why?
- When I am having a good day, which of my friends or colleagues can turn my outlook from upbeat to gloomy or, worse, antagonistic? What is the common factor in what these people say or do?

- What situations or individuals trigger feelings of vulnerability or helplessness—and the desire to defend myself to them and to others?
- Are there some individuals I tell *others* I would like to give a piece of my mind? Why?

Be honest with yourself. If there are others in your life—in the office or at home—who don't appreciate everything you do for them, and that fact always gets to you, recognize that this is one of your hot buttons. If your boss always compliments one of your co-workers but never acknowledges your contributions, although they often exceed the other person's, and you think it unfair, and often complain about it to colleagues, then this is another hot button. One way we respond to a situation or person who triggers our hot button is to talk about the circumstance or individual incessantly.

Ian, a marketing assistant, couldn't tolerate his boss's indecisiveness. One day, Linda wanted something done a certain way; the very next day, after Ian had already begun the job, Linda would change her mind and ask him to do the task otherwise. After each such occurrence, Ian couldn't seem to put the situation to rest; he would talk about Linda with anyone on staff who was sympathetic, then think about the situation all evening long.

Finally, one day, when Ian was asked by Linda to redo the graphics on a report, although it actually involved little extra work, he lost control, shouted "I quit," and grabbing his coat from the clothes closet left the office floor and went home.

Linda had pressed his hot button one time too much. After the situation, like many who have responded on an unconscious level rather than on a rational basis to a situation, Ian couldn't understand why he had quit. But the die was cast. Had he looked inside himself to find out why her indecisiveness so irritated him and how his response to her behavior reflected his own needs—the second step in anger control—(1) he might have discussed the problem with Linda much sooner, and consequently (2) the problem would not have reached the point where emotionally he could no longer take another instance of her indecisiveness.

Aside from the extra work Linda caused him, why did Ian react as he did? Had Ian given it some consideration, he might have realized that he was envious of her position. Although he was her assistant, Ian was the same age as Linda; he also had worked for the company the same number of years as Linda. The job required a master's degree, and she had one and he didn't. Because of the need for the extra sheep skin, she had ended up his boss, which he felt she didn't deserve, not only because of her indecisiveness but due to other management mistakes she would make in the course of a day.

For the purpose of anger control, he had to stop trying to prove himself right—that is, that she didn't deserve the job of his boss—and move beyond blaming her to acceptance of the situation or to identifying the source of her indecisiveness and looking with her for a way to work more productively with her.

The process is reminiscent of the Irish prayer: "God grant me the serenity to accept those things I can't change, the courage to change those I can change, and the wisdom to know the difference." In management terms, we need to know what is behind our feelings, what we can control and what we can't, and work with the person with whom we have a difference to find a mutually satisfactory solution, assuming that there is one.

If there is no workable solution, we need to learn to laugh at the behavior with a friend rather than obsess with him or her about what happened. At the very least, since continually hearing about one issue from you can slowly wear out the patience of even the best of friends, think of this remedy as a means of maintaining existing friendships. Learn to flow with such situations rather than let them make you tense and irritable with others.

In Ian's case, he could have used his management know-how to address the problem with Linda. Instead of accepting each change without comment, he could have asked why she was reversing earlier decisions. If he could have identified the kinds of issues she often didn't consider when she gave him instructions, he could have raised such concerns casually when she gave him projects to be sure that she had given these issues consideration. While it might not have eliminated the problem entirely, it might have minimized the frequency of occurrences.

He could also have saved himself extra work if he considered the dynamics in the department. He might have realized that Linda often reviewed her decisions with her own supervisor, and many times that supervisor countermanded her choices. All Ian needed to do to avoid having to undo work already done was to wait before starting a project for Linda to discuss it with Henry.

The Other Side of the Story

Some readers may think that I'm suggesting that we allow ourselves to be walked over by those in positions above us or otherwise give in to people rather than confront an issue. Not so. As you will see in the next chapter, I believe that there are ways to pro-actively address conflicts just as there are various ways to reactively address conflicts. The point here, however, is that we need to look at the contribution we make to conflicts and address this in a controlled fashion.

There may even be occasions when we want to show anger to make clear to another how upset we truly are about an issue. The key, however, is not to allow our anger to control us. We're talking here about *utilizing anger to demonstrate the importance of an issue to us, and communicating that anger in an assertive manner, rather than in an aggressive or confrontational manner.*

How to Use Anger

We have all felt anger at one time or another at a co-worker or a boss, but generally we try to hide our feelings. We think we're helping the situation, when in truth holding in our feelings about an incident only means that the other party has no way of knowing that there is something wrong.

For instance, in the case of Linda and Ian, Linda, unlike all of Ian's friends, had no idea that Ian was upset with her, although she might have suspected that something was wrong in her work relationship with him.

When it comes to anger, we have three options: hide our anger, yell and scream, or practice controlled disagreement.

We can hide our anger either because we don't want to hurt the other person's feelings or we are concerned about the negative repercussions. Despite the provocations some of our bosses might give us, for instance, how many of us would feel secure in giving our emotions free rein and telling our boss off? Yet not doing so doesn't allow us to address the problem; furthermore, when we bottle up our anger, it can have a physical effect on us, causing anything from ulcers to high blood pressure.

Alternatively, we can yell and scream—but generally such behavior only makes us look overly emotional and unprofessional. Others see us and consider us out of control and sympathize with the person to whom we directed our anger. No matter how justified our outburst, that individual ends up getting away with her behavior; we suffer rather than the other person. The person denies the validity of your argument or tries to make you feel guilty for your unbecoming behavior. Certainly little gets done about the problem itself. The individual may give in this time but over the longer term we can expect an attempt to get even. Lois lost her temper once with a colleague, and thereafter, whenever Lois disagreed with Martin about an issue in team meetings, he would laugh and say, "Look out. Lois is angry. Stand clear—she's going to lose control and yell."

Controlled disagreement is the best way to deal with differences that rile you up. Rather than show your anger, controlled disagreement has you expressing your feelings of anger: "I feel angry because . . . ."

Not only do you tell the other person that you feel angry but you explain the reason(s) for your feelings, like "I feel angry because you don't keep me informed about developments on a project that directly affects my job." Beyond this, you let the person know what he could do to eliminate the provocation for anger, like "If you included me among those who receive minutes from our project meetings or, better yet, include me in these meetings, not only would I be better prepared to act upon the decisions made but I could contribute my knowledge of the area to the discussion."

This approach clearly has advantages over the previous two:

1. You get to express your feelings without destroying your image of professionalism.

2. You get to express the problem—and, if you can, offer a solution to which the other person would be amenable.

3. If you were clear about the reason behind your feelings of anger, a recurrence of the situation is unlikely.

4. The person may not agree with you about the seriousness of the disagreement or even accept your recommended solution but she should respect your honesty about the situation. If you and she have deeper problems between you, and your expression of feelings is unlikely to change that, you still have not given your nemesis ammunition to use against you with other people.

5. Whether you win or lose about the issue itself, expressing your feelings can have a more healthful effect on you than either smothering them or blasting them out.

If you have had a history of anger-provoking incidents with someone, or your temperament is such that you are easily provoked to anger, you may think that controlled disagreement is too difficult for you to master. Not so. I know of one assistant whose only honest and open communications with her boss were when they both were screaming at each other. Allison's boss was a practitioner of verbal abuse, and while Allison made every effort to stay calm during these incidents, periodically her anger would burst through her British reserve and she would scream and even swear at her boss. When these incidents occurred in public, her boss would glare then walk away. But if they happened in the privacy of her boss's office, he would lose his temper. Individuals in the hallways could hear these confrontations.

To some extent, these explosive discussions cleared the air. That is, for awhile, Allison did not suffer from her boss's rude comments about her competency. She, in turn, treated him with the respect his position demanded. One problem: These sessions never dealt with the main issue, which was that Allison's boss was taking his professional and/or personal problems out on his assistant.

It wasn't until Allison learned to practice something called "emotional disengaging" that she was able to hold back her anger and assertively discuss with her boss her feelings about his remarks. Emotional disengaging entails teaching yourself to look upon the anger-provoking situation as a stranger might look upon it, rather than as a participant. No question, this isn't easy to do; it requires that you put your emotions in neutral at the same time you are frustrated or angry, or hurt. However, practice over time will enable you to put the incident in perspective and control the intensity of your emotional response. In Allison's case, it meant that the hurtful words from her boss no longer had the power to destroy her self-esteem or otherwise make her feel violated. She felt sufficiently in control to speak coolly but calmly her feelings about his comments. When her boss did nothing about the situation, she was able to bring the matter to the human resources department and also make her case in a thoughtful and rational manner. Her boss was reprimanded, and he eventually left.

Allison and her new boss have a good working relationship.

How can you develop this kind of detachment to enable you to cope with a conflict-producing difference? Statements repeated over time can put your mind in the right frame. Here are some affirmations that can build self-esteem and enable you to see situations from perspectives other than your own and, in the process, enable you to control your anger, since anger is often a product of both low self-esteem and a self-centeredness:

- Every day and in every way I'm getting better and better.
- It's okay to make mistakes so long as I learn from them.
- I have strengths, and I know it.
- I'm not responsible for making others happy.
- I am calm and in control.

Assertive Communications

Keep in mind that Allison was able to communicate *assertively* her side of the matter, first, with her boss and, later, with the HR department.

When I meet with office professionals, either they tell me that they find it hard to speak assertively or they assure me that they practice assertive behavior, but further discussion generally indicates otherwise. They see as an assertive person someone who pushes her own way, refusing to give an inch, adamant about her view of an issue, whereas assertive behavior is nothing more than being direct and respectful when interacting with others. I remember an office professional telling me, "I can be assertive when I have to be." Which I translated to mean, "I can be tough if I have to be." This isn't assertive behavior.

Most people are nonassertive or apologetic or hesitant, or they are aggressive or accusatory or blameful. But when you are nonassertive, people will walk over you. If you are aggressive, you invite defensiveness from others. Only assertiveness invites cooperation.

Since nonassertiveness and aggressive behavior can stem from a negative self-image or self-centeredness, the affirmations listed earlier will help you to develop or strengthen your assertive behavior and, consequently, give you the communication skills you need to prevent a difference from developing into a conflict. You have to change your feelings toward yourself before you can comfortably change your behavior, which includes not only how you speak to others but also what words you choose.

Throughout this book you will read about how body language can trigger conflict or defuse it. Voice tone, inflection, pace, eye contact or lack of it, facial expressions, gestures, movements or not, and posture all send signals to another party. Shoulders slumped forward or a chin down is nonassertive body language. Nervous laughter and frequent nodding of the head are also indicative of nonassertiveness. If these behaviors are accompanied with averted eyes or a guilty look, the person is angry but unable to express that anger because of self-esteem and other issues.

I recently attended a manager meeting with a staff member. The organization is going through downsizing, and the staff member was asking his boss if he was on the list of those who would be downsized. The boss muttered that he didn't know anything and moved on. Based on his body language, it was evident to me—and to the staff member—that his boss knew more than he was willing to say. "I'd better clean my resume off," the wise staff member said as he watched his boss, slumped forward with a guilty look on his face, shuffle away.

Aggressive body language is also easy to identify. Soldier-like aggressive people stand with shoulders back in a tense posture. Their chin is thrust forward. Their fists are clenched. As they speak, their chin nods up and down quickly. When they are angered, they may scowl; their mouth becomes firm and they speak between clenched teeth like a friend of mine when he gets angry. He seems almost to be biting his words; a professional speaker like myself, he becomes more precise as he speaks. Like many, he has overcompensated—moving from a nonassertive style as a youth to an aggressive manner as he went into the consulting business. He's working to develop an assertive manner, in which his voice is smooth and its tone is even-flowing.

He still needs to stand straight but he should look more relaxed and less rigid. His hands should be open with the palms out rather than clenched. Instead of being steely quiet when he's angry (aggressive) or letting his voice hit a high pitch (nonassertive), he needs to control it so his voice is firm but pleasant. And he should stop giggling.

But what you say is just as important as how you look when you say it. Your words mustn't convey a "must-win" attitude anymore than your body language. This means avoiding the following don'ts:

- Don't say "you should" or "you must." Rather, when asking someone whose comments are provoking you to stop, say, "Will you please . . . ?"

- Don't use "you" statements. Rather, switch to "I" statements, such as "I would like to tell you why I disagree with your plan" when your boss continually interrupts you instead of hearing you out (while your temper, meanwhile, is rising).

- Don't exaggerate or make judgments about a co-worker's actions. Rather, focus on the facts. Consequently, you don't want to say to your colleague, "You're going to be in big trouble if you don't help me with this work." Rather, tell her, "If you continue to leave at 4:00

or 4:30, we won't be able to complete your work and mine. And these letters must go out to all our clients by this Friday. Our manager is expecting us to complete the mailing by noon."

- Don't say, "I can't" or "I won't be able to do it." Those are conflict trigger-phrases in response to requests from your boss. Rather, say assertively, which means politely and firmly, "No," then go on to explain why not.

- Don't say, "Andy makes me angry when he . . . ," when explaining to a third party, perhaps the human resources manager (remember Allison), why some incident or person upsets you. Say, instead, "I get angry when . . . ." Assertive people make clear to others their feelings by taking ownership for them.

- Don't throw adverbs around such as "never," "always," "generally," and the like. Not only are such words usually exaggerations of the facts, which weakens your case, they are also trigger-words likely to upset someone. Rather, stick to the facts. As Allison told human resources, "On three occasions over the last two weeks, my boss called me incompetent, blaming me for mistakes that others were responsible for."

- Don't be vague. If you want to state your thoughts, even though they reflect a difference in thinking from your boss, a co-worker, or customer, say, "I think . . . ." If you want to share your opinion with one of those individuals, even if they have very strong opinions to the contrary, say politely but clearly, "I believe . . . ." If you want to express your feelings, like anger because of someone's indifference to your feelings, say, "I feel angry . . ." or "I am angry when . . . ."

The last is very important. People don't generally express their emotions openly. When you do so, you can get the attention of the person with whom you are talking and on the brink of having a conflict. Besides telling someone specifically about your feelings—"You're getting me angry by . . . ."—you can emphasize key words to express the state of your emotion (for example, "*Please* let me finish my statement. I think that when you *let me express my concern*, you will understand why I have doubts about this change in office procedures.").

Repetition is another means of expressing growing anger without showing it. If you have eye contact with the other person, you send a clear message to the individual that you are upset and the situation can grow out of control if the person isn't responsive to your statement or query. Likewise, when you add to your requests or comments statements of what you intend to do if you don't get cooperation or help with your request (or if the person continues to be anger-provoking), the individual is more likely to be cooperative or to end her anger-provoking behavior. Remember when you were a child and a sibling or friend taunted you and you said, "I am upset. If you keep taking my toys, I'm going to tell . . . .", the other youngster stopped misbehaving. Assertiveness works the same way: "If I don't have your time sheet before the end of the day, I am afraid that I will have to report to human resources your failure to submit it. I am angry that I have to tell you each day . . . ."

Talking the Problem Out

The last statement was actually made by Millie to Hermine. Millie is assistant to the vice president of marketing. Hermine reports to Todd, one of the marketing managers who reports to Fran. One of Millie's responsibilities is to report weekly attendance to human resources. Forms have been developed, and each assistant in the department is expected to complete it and return it by mid-day on Friday. Failure to do it by then can create paperwork problems in human resources, which has to prepare a final report by the end of Friday and send it to the firm's payroll offices, which are located at another facility. Millie and Hermine got along well until Fran put Millie in charge of the division's administrative council, a group of assistants whose function is to identify administrative opportunities for continuous improvement. Fran had read about the concept in a business magazine and had decided to set up a council in her division. If it worked there, she planned to recommend a companywide initiative.

The problem was that Hermine, a corporate veteran unlike Millie, felt herself more familiar with the division's operation—indeed, the entire company's—than Millie. Hermine thought that she, not Millie, should have been made head of the council. Two of the three other assistants felt likewise, but they were willing to go along with Millie's appointment. At meetings, Hermine also was cooperative. But over little things, like getting the attendance sheet in on time or seeing that copies of trade journals went directly to Fran after Todd saw them, Hermine dragged her feet.

The first time Hermine turned in the attendance report late, Millie was understanding. But after she had to come to Hermine three weeks in a row to get the report, she knew that Hermine was deliberately holding back the report to make Millie's job more difficult. While Hermine's act of rebellion was small, it began increasingly to upset Millie because it meant one more thing that she had to do on an already busy Friday. Besides, it was very important for Millie to prove to Fran how well she could manage others—she had hopes of eventually convincing Fran that she needed her own assistant. Yes, Hermine had found Millie's hot button.

Fortunately for Hermine—Millie told me that one day, given all the rest of the "stuff 'n things" she had on her desk, she felt like punching out Hermine for adding to her work—Millie decided to use controlled disagreement assertive communications to talk out their problem. Toward that, she:

- Played up the importance of her relationship with her co-worker. Millie set the stage for the problem solving by saying, "I have always valued our relationship. I appreciate your support at the administrative council."
- Stated the nature of the problem. Millie then went on to explain the ongoing problem. "I am angry," she said, "that each Friday I have to remind you that I need the attendance report by noon."
- Asked Hermine's side of the problem. Millie went on to inquire of Hermine, "Why do you think getting the report to me is a problem for you?" Then, Millie continued, "What do you think we should do about the situation?" Hermine scowled at her, but Millie kept her own anger in check and stated assertively, "If I don't get these reports on schedule, I will have to talk to Fran and Todd about the problem to ensure that payroll gets the information it needs on time." Millie then:

- Made an offer. "To help solve the problem, I am willing to discuss the issue with the human resources department to see if we can turn in the reports later, say by mid-afternoon."
- Asked for what she wanted. Millie then asked Hermine if she could get the report to her by 2 P.M. on Friday. Otherwise, she would have to report the situation to the head of marketing and the human resources department.

Throughout the conversation, Millie kept her voice on an even level. She sat at ease at her desk and looked at Hermine seated across from her. Hermine knew that Millie could have demanded that she get the reports to her by noon, or otherwise put her in the wrong. Hermine knew that Millie had every reason to lose her temper but, instead, it seemed to Hermine—and correctly—that Millie was trying to address not only the issue of the attendance reports but their work relationship as well.

Hermine promised to get the reports to Millie by noon. In doing so, she was also promising to work toward rebuilding her relationship with Millie.

What if Hermine had been ready to fight instead of collaborate with Millie? In the next chapter, you will discover how to identify others' hot buttons and what tactics besides problem solving you can use to deal with a difference before it becomes a conflict.

3

Pro-Active Solutions

Just as there are issues that can upset you, so, too, there are issues that can upset the people with whom you work. Some comment or action on your part could put you and another party—boss, co-worker, or customer, for instance—in a conflict unless you defuse the situation. Or you could find yourself asked by two co-workers to mediate a conflict between them.

You can't prevent conflicts from arising, but you can reduce their frequency if you:

- **Show understanding for a person's outlook, position, frustration, and/or predicament.** Angry words are often an effort to get another person's attention.
- **Ask questions.** When we listen to another person, without interrupting, we can better understand where the individual is coming from. Many hostile exchanges stem from failure to hear what someone is saying. If you can anticipate a difference, you can address it more diplomatically.
- **Stop talking.** If you said something, and you find the person with whom you are talking becoming upset and continually interrupting you, then something you have said has upset the person. Pause. The silence that follows should help the other person regain control; then you can probe to find the source of the problem.
- **Repeat some of the person's key phrases and ideas.** Your intention is to determine what you said or did to rile the person. So keep your tone one of interest, not judgment. Say, you made a comment about a co-worker's attire, either because it's too formal for a dress-down day or too informal for one. You thought you were being tactful but you clearly offended. You had made mention of the outfit, then

continued on about another issue, but your colleague kept going back to her wardrobe. She had said, "I'm not going to be ridiculed in front of others for the way I dress at the office." You might want to backtrack and ask, "Ridiculed?" then pause. Your co-worker will elaborate: "Well, you just told me in front of several of my friends that you think I look like a slob, didn't you?"

You would then repeat the word "slob," and pause again.

Once you have insights into what is bothering the other person, you are in a position to diplomatically address the issue. Did you mean that the person was dressed inappropriately? Or is the individual misinterpreting your words? If it's the former, you need to clarify your comment. If it's the latter, you need to decide if you want to address your differences in perspective about what is appropriate apparel for a dress-down day, or simply apologize for offending your co-worker.

Hot Buttons

How do you know what issues can upset another person? As you read in Chapter 2, hot buttons take many forms, from values and beliefs, to situations, people, and events, to deep-rooted emotional vulnerabilities like lack of self-esteem or a need to be liked, or a desire to be in control. You may work with someone for many years yet never know what could rile this person enough to make it difficult, if not impossible, to work with him. That you have upset him, on the other hand, should be clearly evident. He may turn red and angry and draw you back to the source of his upset, or he may turn on his heels and walk away and be curt with you in the future, refusing to return your telephone calls or respond to your e-mail. If the person works for you, he may go around slamming stacks of paper or making other unnecessary noise.

If you have yet to exchange harsh words, however, you may be able to return to your previous relationship if you take some action as soon as possible. Your response depends on the person's communication style and the situation, in addition to the importance of your work relationship with this individual. But the more important the work relationship, the more immediate the action you should take.

Preventing Conflicts

Let me give you an example. Loretta is an office professional. When she gets upset with someone, if that person tries to mend fences, that person has a tough time because Loretta will trash that person, hurling words as if each one was a four-letter word. She's very temperamental, and bringing up any problem with her is like opening up a dam of hurt feelings.

If you are dealing with someone like Loretta, then you need to stay calm and in control until she has fully vented. If you let her words upset you, you could quickly move into the shouting stage and a full-blown conflict.

Prepare in advance answers to the accusations that will be hurled in your direction. Keep your tone of voice even; if you raise your voice, you are likely to escalate the discussion from disagreement to conflict to outright war.

If you inadvertently press a Loretta-like person's hot button, and he immediately reacts, your best response is to withdraw temporarily until the person has calmed down. Or you might try a diplomatic approach, trying to smooth the waters.

With either approach, you should stick to the facts. This individual wants a shouting match, which will only take yours and the other person's differences to the next level. You want to bring the conflict down a level to an unbiased discussion of the situation.

Mel isn't like Loretta. He's a whiner, continuously griping about a situation that he blames on you. Mel is more likely to build a faction against you than direct his complaint to you. If you want to avoid the rest of the staff ganging up on you or the department taking sides, you have to say something to Mel and put an end to his moanings. If your boss is acting like Mel, you could have a serious problem if the complaint isn't addressed, since it could find its way into your performance appraisal.

When you try to handle differences between you and a Mel-like person, it is most important that you don't become defensive. Stay objective, like a diplomat. Whereas with a Loretta-type, you would be the person offering specifics to explain what happened, when dealing with a Mel-like person you should be asking for specifics. Once you have the facts, you can then move the discussion back to the issue that triggered the disagreement and stay there.

Some of those with whom you work may fall into a third category, flip-flopping by first calmly responding to a difference between you, then switching over and acting heated about the situation. Anne is like that, as her supervisor discovered. Pat, an office assistant, had known Anne for some years; when Pat received approval to hire an assistant for herself, she asked Anne if she would transfer from purchasing to take the job. Since Pat had been a little insecure about her first supervisory responsibility, she was delighted when Anne agreed. Pat felt her friendship with Anne would make her task easier.

Not so. If Pat complained about some task that Anne had done poorly, Anne would look upset and apologize for the mistake. But shortly thereafter, Anne would make a comment that suggested that she thought Pat had really been to blame for the mistake.

It was Pat who felt like yelling but it was Anne who was building the situation to the point of a conflict. Fortunately, Pat knew that yelling would only escalate the difference—and lead to tears on Anne's part. Anne would apologize while sniffling into a tissue, then once again she would say something that suggested that the incident was Pat's fault.

Anne would also tell others what had happened and gain sympathy from the rest of the staff.

Pat eventually rid herself of Anne, due to Anne's poor performance. But in the interim, she learned how to handle the near conflicts between her and Anne. When Anne would aggressively retract her initial acknowledgment that she was at fault, Pat would calmly cite the specific mistakes that Anne had made. If there was written evidence that Anne had made a mistake, Pat would show that to her. She learned to ignore the conflict-inducing behavior on Anne's part, and focus instead on the work that had to be done. Although withdrawing until a Loretta-type has cooled off is the best tactic there, and a diplomatic approach is best in dealing with a Mel-type, using a directive style (based on one's position of authority) is most effective with an Anne-type.

While Anne was on staff, Pat knew that Anne was telling tales about her to the rest of the staff; but she also knew that most of the staff admired Pat's patience with Anne.

Let me tell you about another situation involving an office professional with an assistant. Jennie is a temp and comes in three days a week. She wants a full-time job, and Barbara wouldn't mind having Jennie as a full-time assistant except that Jennie has a problem: she's great with assignments that call for creativity and offer high visibility, whereas she acts as if she left her brains at home when she's given routine tasks. When Barbara insists she do a task, Jennie sulks as she works or, worse, becomes obstreperous until no one in the office can work because of Jennie's chatter to one and all.

A collaborative approach ultimately worked here. Barbara took Jennie out to lunch, and during the meal she asked her about her career goals. When she learned that Jennie wanted to work full time at the company, Barbara pointed out that she, then, was doing a disservice to herself by her behavior. Barbara explained that she wanted a full-time assistant and that she thought Jennie might fit into the role but, Barbara continued, it was unlikely that she would get that opportunity unless she showed Barbara how valuable she could be. And both women demonstrated how Jennie working for Barbara would allow Barbara to get so much more administrative work done. That meant that Jennie would have to handle mundane tasks with the same enthusiasm she showed when she took on more challenging work.

The discussion had the effect Barbara wanted. Since cooperating with Barbara would get Jennie what she wanted, she accepted the need to collaborate. Barbara, in turn, looked for opportunities for Jennie to show her full abilities. In the end both got what they wanted: Barbara got a full-time assistant, Jennie.

Addressing Someone's Anger with You

Of all the many techniques to prevent a difference from degenerating into a conflict, negotiation can be particularly effective, especially if the other person is already at the angry stage and has begun to shout. Before you begin negotiating, you have to deal with this individual's anger. Toward that, you will have to hear the person out without losing your own temper. Listening isn't just letting your boss or a colleague or a customer blow off steam. It entails really trying to understand what the person is angry about. Suggest that the person move from the present environment into another environment and then sit down with the person to hear him out.

As the person talks:

- **Don't interrupt.** When you interrupt, you are telling a speaker that you aren't really listening. You've already prejudged the person and you see no reason to hear him out.
- **Don't move beyond what the person is saying.** Don't let your imagination take the problem beyond what the other party is saying. For instance, don't assume that your boss plans to fire you if he's angry that you made a mistake on a customer's order. And don't jump ahead with an angry friend to assume that you both will never lunch together.
- **Watch what your body is saying.** Eye contact and body posture are nonverbal ways you tell the other person that you are truly listening to their complaint.
- **Paraphrase.** Don't merely repeat what you heard in your own words. Ask the person if you are accurate in understanding his complaint.
- **Show a willingness to understand.** When the angry individual tells you, "You don't understand," and you respond, "Of course I do," you may escalate the anger rather than calming the person. A more appropriate response might be, "I want to understand."
- **Recognize that the stated complaint may not be the underlying reason for the outburst.** The real problem may have to do with another situation, person, or event. If you suspect this to be the case, probe more deeply to get the person to expand on her comments.
- **Avoid observations that make the person more defensive.** As you search for the source of the person's anger, avoid comments that might produce further hurt feelings. Say, "I'm sorry, but I really don't understand your comment . . . ."

Continue to ask questions and then backtrack to clarify points until you feel you have a sense of the true source of this difference that could become a conflict between you and the person in the future.

Once you understand the nature of the problem, you are ready to discuss how the situation can be remedied. If it is possible to do as the person requests, do so. You might also want to apologize if you find that you were in the wrong. Maybe your expectation from your boss was unrealistic? Or you are failing to realize that your co-workers have their own long to-do lists to complete, and that's why they can't help you, as you expected them to do.

What if the person wants you to do something that is impossible for you to do? This is when negotiation comes in.

Agreeing to do something, even though you know you can't or won't, will only provoke a repeat of the scene and perhaps escalate the feelings of anger from the other person. Keep in mind that it is critical that the angry colleague or boss has to have trust in your willingness to resolve the difference. Only then can you ensure that it won't develop into a full-blown conflict that could cost you your job if the angry individual is your boss or erode your job satisfaction and increase the stress you feel if it's a colleague.

Negotiations

Once you agree to enter into negotiations, keep these points in mind:

- **Set some preconditions.** You want to set the stage for a collaborative resolution of the disagreement. Toward that goal, you have to demonstrate why both you and the other party have a stake in the negotiation process—that more can be gained by negotiating than by continuing to argue over the issue. Toward that end, encourage the other party to identify the goals or objectives she wants to achieve. Do the same.
- **Recognize the legitimacy of the other person's needs.** Behaving as if the other party has no right to feeling as she does, or the right to ask for what she is asking, guarantees a deadlock.
- **Don't play at negotiation.** In other words, be sincere about your desire to find a solution that is acceptable to you and the other party. Which means that you have to be willing to take the time that negotiation may take. Don't sell the process short. Don't do as some

people do, by giving in for the moment, agreeing to the other party's demands, even though you have no intention of delivering on your promises.

Such behavior can make you lose the trust not only of the party with whom you are negotiating but also of everyone with whom you work.

- **Adequately prepare.** Based on the source of the contention between you and the other person, you may want to take some time to prepare for the negotiation. The problem with playing a negotiation session by ear is that the final conclusions reached are ones you probably won't want to hear.

  Toward preparation, you may want to ask yourself these questions:

  —Is there more than one possible solution to the problem—my solution?

  —Is there any solution that I know I couldn't live with?

  —How will I demonstrate the impossibility of that solution to the other party?

  —Am I sure that I have identified all solutions that I could live with?

  —Can I present my solution in a manner that will increase the likelihood of the upset person's acceptance?

  —How can my answer be made acceptable to the other person?

- **Refocus your mindset toward a win-win conclusion.** While no solution truly allows each person to walk away 100 percent satisfied, this should be your goal. When you enter into a negotiation to defuse a disagreement, think in terms of resolving the problem rather than winning. It's not you versus the other person but rather you trying to come to grips with a difference that needs to be resolved for the positive relationship with the other person to resume. A win-lose mindset is baggage likely to forestall any workable solution coming out of the session.

- **Watch your language.** The way you phrase your ideas is as important as your ideas during the negotiation. For instance, don't say:

  —"You don't understand." In the other person's mind, you may have just told her that she is too stupid to understand.

  —"It can't be done that way." Rather, say, "Have you considered . . . . ?"

—"How could you say . . . . ?" That's a guilt trick that will only alienate the other person further.

—"That's beside the point." Even if the comment is irrelevant, when you say this while the other person is speaking during negotiations, you are telling him that you want total control of the discussion. Better to let the individual express his thought then bring him back on track.

- **Stay professional.** The other person may not be able to keep her emotions under control. No matter how sarcastic or otherwise abrasive the other person is, stay calm. In fact, if you behave in a professional manner, it's likely that the other party will likewise do so.
- **Don't look back, look forward.** Don't defend yourself by dredging up slights from the other person in the past that you had overlooked. Instead, encourage a focus on the future and improved relationships.
- **Put yourself in the other person's shoes.** Consider carefully what the other person is saying. You may think that the other person is making much ado about nothing, but keep in mind that two people can assess a situation very differently. This is particularly true when the anger is tied to one of our hot buttons. Keeping this in mind is apt to make you more objective during negotiations and less likely to act pigheaded about your stance.
- **Direct the discussion to new behaviors.** This is a key to resolving the problem between you and the other person. You both have to decide how to prevent a recurrence of the situation that brought you into negotiation. What will you do to maintain a more positive relationship? What will you expect from the other person in kind? [Here's where your preparation comes in.] If the upset is due to an omission or commission on your part, admit your mistake and ask, "What can I do to make it up to you?"
- **Keep your promise.** Each time we promise but then fail to do as we offered, we lose a little of the respect of others, until we have none left.

Mediation

Some conflicts demand the assistance of a third party to help the disputants resolve the conflict. If you remain flexible in seeking a solution to a conflict through negotiation, and follow the advice above, it's unlikely that you will have to ask a fellow worker, manager, or member of human resources to mediate. More likely, you may be asked to mediate between other co-workers who aren't able to resolve their differences.

Should that occur, you will have to go through the five-step process with the parties to the dispute:

- **Identify the source of their conflict.** The more information you have about the conflict, the more you can help your colleagues resolve their differences. To get the information you need, you can use a series of questions very similar to those that you would ask a person you were conflicting with, such as "When did you first feel upset?" "Do you see a relationship between that event and these subsequent feelings toward your co-worker?" "How did this argument begin?"

  As mediator, your objective is to give both parties to the conflict an opportunity to share their side of the story. This will enable you to better understand the nature of the situation, as well as prove your impartiality in the conflict. As you listen to each disputant, demonstrate that you are actively listening to the words by nodding your head and periodically saying "I see" or "Uh huh."

- **Look beyond the incident.** As I said earlier, often it isn't a specific situation but one's perspective on the situation that causes anger to fester and ultimately leads to a shouting match or other visible—and disruptive—evidence of a conflict.

  As you may discover when you look into conflicts in which you are a participant, you may find that the source of the conflict between the two disputants is a minor problem that occurred months before, but that the level of stress has grown to the point where the two individuals have begun to attack each other personally instead of addressing the real issue.

  As mediator, you may get the two individuals to identify the real cause of their difficulty and address it. Toward this, you may want to ask: "What do you think happened here?" Or, "When do you think a problem between you two first began?"

- **Look for solutions.** After you have each party's perspective on the conflict, the next step is to have each identify how the situation could be changed. Your goal, again, is to get the disputants to share their opinions: "How can you make things better between you?"

  Listen to their responses. Look for solutions that would steer the discussion away from fingerpointing and toward a resolution of the differences between the disputants.

- **Identify answers that both parties can support.** You want to identify the course of action that is most acceptable to both parties and, as important, truly doable. You want an answer to the following questions: "What action plan can you both put in place to prevent a similar conflict arising between you?" "What will you do if a problem arises in the future?"

  You want to reach the kind of accord where the answer to the latter question is, "Discuss it."

- **Reach agreement.** As mediator for your colleagues, you want to reach the point where they are able to shake hands and agree to one of the solutions that were identified in the discussions. To be sure that the two understand each other, it might be wise for each to paraphrase what the other has agreed to, in your presence.

A Point Worth Commenting on

If you think about the remedies proposed in Section I of this book, repeatedly you will find mention of three points critical to addressing conflicts:

1. **Make an effort to understand the other person's views.** Whether you are upset with another person or that person is angry with you, or you are mediating between two co-workers at war, the same advice is applicable. You need to hear out the other person. Ask why she thinks that way. Even paraphrase what was said to be sure that you understand. It doesn't mean that you agree, only that you now know where the other individual is coming from.

2. **Look for a basis of agreement.** You may not agree with the other person's viewpoint, but you need some starting point for

discussion. It may be solely that the other person is upset by your behavior or you are angered by hers. Don't dredge up past grievances. Rather, acknowledge a problem and a need to improve your relationship.

3. **Seek answers.** The third and final step is to show your willingness to close the gap in thinking or otherwise eliminate the differences between you. This means identifying a solution that is acceptable to both of you.

In the next section of the book, we will look at three major causes of conflicts and how you can avoid the traps they represent or, if you do find yourself in one, how to resolve the conflict it caused.

Section II

Getting to the Heart of a Problem

4

Communication Gaffes

Many conflicts are a product of communication or, actually, miscommunication, if you think of communication as a process in which an idea or thought is conveyed to another person. Too often the messages we send are unclear. They are poorly worded or sent with body language that refutes our words. Just as often, those to whom we send these messages are preoccupied with thoughts of how to respond and consequently don't hear us. Or they are listening to our words through a personal filter made up of their viewpoint that blocks our idea or thought. Or we don't listen to those with whom we have a conflict and consequently have no sense of the conflict's cause.

So how do you communicate effectively? Let's look at this simple four-part formula for effective communications:

1. Be sure that you have the attention of the other person. Find a time to speak to the person when she isn't distracted with other concerns, even if you must make an appointment to talk, which may be the case with a busy boss. How can you be sure that a time is right to speak with another person? Ask, "Do you have a moment to talk to me?"
2. Explain your position, situation, or idea to your colleague or manager in a clear and comprehensible manner. Keep emotion out of your voice as well as out of your statement. Stick to the facts. To ensure that the other person is following your comments, check periodically: "Am I making myself clear?" "Have I made my case clear?" (Don't ask the other party, "Do you understand what I am suggesting?" or a similar question because such phrasing

implies that the other person is unable to keep up with your comments.)

3. Be alert to body language. Stance, arm gestures, and facial expression send a message as clear as words and voice tone. You don't want to talk to a co-worker about a more collaborative work relationship while at the same time the tone of your voice and your body is telling him that you feel forced to work with the person.

4. Be sure that your message has been received. Frequently, you will be able to tell by the person's response if she got it. A hot, heated response is a clear indicator that the person didn't get your message, that the message you sent did not get through to the person because the individual's personal filter blocked the message, or that the message you sent was unclear, perhaps distorted by unclear body language or warped by your own filters (values and beliefs).

The Art of Communication

The four-part formula above reflects the importance of three elements in any communications you send, in writing or in person:

1. **Content.** Beyond being clear, your communications should be rational, specific, and direct. The more they are, the less likely there will be a misunderstanding that ends in a conflict.

   A written message should not leave its recipient confused or, worse, hurt. Sensitive issues should be handled with tact. Admittedly, we have so much to do during the day that taking extra time to perfect even small notes may seem a waste of time, but consider the after-effect from sending a message that either confuses and leads to a mistake or one that offends and leads to hostile feelings, which makes your future work relationship difficult.

   This warning is particularly important when sending e-mail. You can plant the seed for a growing conflict inadvertently by a poor choice of words. Minimize confusion by supplementing such written communications as e-mail and meeting minutes with face-to-face communications.

   The same advice applies to verbal communications. Follow up one-on-one meetings with brief notes that summarize conclusions reached.

Although one-on-one verbal communications would seem less prone to confusion, this is not so. Most individuals are reluctant to ask for clarification about instructions or a comment even though the person giving the instructions or making the comment is standing right beside them. Whereas some written communications suffer from information overload, many verbal communications have the opposite problem—a paucity of information, which fails to put the verbal message in perspective, a situation that in today's volatile, and sometimes paranoid, work environments, can trigger feelings of unease and displeasure with the speaker.

Should the content of your communications be a criticism of the recipient or of her work, here's an important tip: Use noninflammatory phrases such as "It seems to me . . . ." or "I feel that . . . ." Don't point a finger by saying, "You don't . . . ." or "You should . . . ." Avoid, too, words such as "always," "never," "generally," and the like, because they damn any efforts by the person and are likely to result in defensive communications in return, which, in turn, can trigger angry outbursts and conflict.

2. **Unclogging communication channels.** Conflicts can arise with someone who has a need for information but who, inadvertently, is not copied on a memo or e-mail message and consequently gets information too late or not at all. It's not a deliberate slight, just a mistake. But it may be hard to convince someone already insecure about her position. The small error can grow until it destroys your working relationship with the person. [Parenthetically, critical messages sent to a colleague, with copies to others in positions of authority, are also likely to alienate and plant the seeds for conflicts in the future.]

3. **Interpersonal relationships.** A warped message or jammed communication pipeline will likely be forgiven if you and the other person already share feelings of trust and mutual self-respect. Toward building the kind of positive relationship that can stand up to tough words, bad news, or being left out of the loop, devote a portion of your time to creating rapport with those with whom you work. Small talk is a good way to begin. Finding common interests can create channels of communication between you and others

with whom cooperative, collaborative relationships are important. People who feel comfortable talking to one another are more likely to discuss differences in a rational manner than those who aren't.

Talking Yourself Out of a Conflict

Let's say that, despite your best communications efforts, anger arises between you and another. How can you resolve the conflict?

The likelihood of such a situation is great in today's highly volatile workplaces where you likely will encounter someone angry at you or something you have done—whether it's a boss, colleague, staff member, or customer. The stress of the work environment has heightened reactions to even the smallest difference in beliefs or values, or reactions to a misunderstanding about some action. Whatever the cause, the person is angry at you, and that anger has to be addressed. Find a quiet place to talk, and then:

- **Acknowledge the person's right to be upset.** Don't ask the person, "Why should you be upset?" Or, "There's no reason to feel like you do." The person shouldn't be asked to justify his feelings. Accept the person's right to feel offended or upset about the difference, then move forward from there to resolve the conflict.
- **Ask questions about the nature of the problem.** The best questions to ask—whether to resolve a conflict in which you are a spectator or one in which you are a participant—are open-ended ones; that is, ask questions that require more than a "yes" or "no" answer as is the case with closed-ended questions.
- **Define the apparent problem.** Both you and the other party should do this. You may discover that you both see the problem from different perspectives. Once you have brought your differences to the surface, you can work toward closing them and then resolving the conflict.
- **Seek out the other person's perspective.** You know what happened. Now you need to see how the parties in the conflict perceive what happened. Compare that with your perception. "How do you feel about what happened?"

- **Analyze the situation.** Once you've determined the nature of the problem, ask the angry party to answer questions like the following:

    —When did the situation become a problem? If so, why didn't the person bring it to your attention? Does the other party feel it is too late to address the problem?

    —Why does the other party think the conflict occurred? Could the conflict have been prevented?

    —How did the conflict occur? What happened that shouldn't have?

    —What can you both do to resolve the conflict?

- **Approach the incident as a problem solving situation.** As the last question suggests, you need to move away from the anger phase toward identification of an answer to the conflict. Remember that personal attacks and blame setting aren't constructive in resolving your differences with this person.

    Solving the problem is easier said than done, of course. Many management books may suggest that it's a simple process: First you open discussion, then the other person speaks, then you speak, and then together you agree on a solution. Fine. Not at all! Depending upon the source of the conflict, the process toward solution can be painful to both of you. Here are some rules to remember as you make that journey together:

    —**Treat the angry person in a polite and courteous manner.** Whenever possible, find an interruption-free place to meet with the person. If the existence of a conflict became evident in a public place, ask the other person to join you in a more private location. An audience won't allow the kind of problem-solving session you need to address the issue.

    —**Give the other party the chance to vent before you move on to the problem solving phase.** You both have to set aside your emotions for this discussion to be productive. As the person vents, don't let yourself react emotionally. Rather, once the person has freed herself of the emotionality associated with the situation, ask, "How can we overcome our problem?"

    —**Listen to the other party's view.** Try to see the situation from the other individual's viewpoint.

—**Be willing to accept and acknowledge your own mistakes; be respectful of the other party when he has admitted mistakes.** Don't ridicule or gloat if a conflicting party accepts your points as valid.

—**Be objective and work toward a cooperative approach.** Don't try to force the other person to accept your position, which means don't try to manipulate the person or use put-downs, know-it-all attitudes, and stubbornness.

—**Avoid observations or questions that may begin the conflict all over again.** You want to move forward, not backward. Put-downs or any other comments that trigger feelings of embarrassment or anxiety are taboo.

—**Encourage a dialogue with the other person.** Don't dominate the conversation. Monologues won't encourage the kind of give and take that will resolve conflicts.

—**Don't make assumptions.** When situations get heated, we sometimes don't communicate explicitly. We jump to conclusions, make faulty assumptions, and try to second-guess another. It is important to spell out all details, ask questions, put agreements in writing, summarize progress, and list agenda items for discussion.

• **Move toward closure.** During the problem solving process, you will be considering alternative solutions to the problem and ultimately selecting one that is acceptable to both you and the other party. You should tell the person: "I think I understand your concern. What can we do to resolve the conflict?"

Sometimes you may discover that you need do nothing more; the person simply needed an opportunity to let off some steam. If that's the case, all you need to do then is say, "I'm glad that we have had an opportunity to talk about this situation. I want to work well with you, and I don't want anything to intervene in our work relationship."

Sometimes the other party will demand some action on your part. If it is outside your authority, acknowledge that. Promise to look into the matter and get back to the person as quickly as you can, if possible by the next day. (And do as you promised: Failure to act as promised will only exacerbate the situation, encouraging the individual to share his complaint about you with others, which can cause factions to develop around the issue.)

If the complaint is a valid one, and you have the authority to act, then do so. And thank the person for bringing the conflict to your attention.

But what if the complaint is invalid and the demand from the other person is unreasonable? All you can say is, "I appreciate your sharing your feelings with me. May I share with you how I see the situation you have presented? Here is the way I see the situation."

Once you've given your explanation, pause to give the other person the opportunity to respond to your remarks. Doing so will give you not only insights into how your explanation is being taken but also proof that the other person grasped your viewpoint. If you find you can't come together on this issue, be mindful that solving this one issue isn't as important as having a positive, friendly, helpful, and fully professional relationship with this person. Consequently, rather than address this specific incident, you may want to return to problem solving—not to resolve the source of this conflict but to identify steps to prevent future conflicts.

How We Say It

As you meet with this individual, be as conscious of what your body is saying as of the words you use. Often, our body language is out of sync with our verbal message. Crossed arms, for instance, are a universal sign of defense. Children often do it when defying adults, and the elderly also do the same when they are insistent on their rights. When you offer to meet with the individual to resolve your conflict, stand near without entering the person's space. Keep your arms open and at your sides.

If you put a hand on your hip, or tap your toe, you are expressing impatience with the person. If one leg is thrust before the other like a boxer's stance, you look ready for a fight.

If you are seated, don't cross your legs; this, like crossed arms, suggests a closed mind to another's ideas. Maintain eye contact. But don't stare, which communicates anger; don't lower your eyes, either—this suggests deceitfulness or disinterest. Watch your body language to be sure that it suggests that you are open to discussion and resolution of the conflict between you and the other person. Watch, too, the other person's body language. If you notice her body language out of sync with what she is saying about her willingness to resolve the conflict—perhaps it suggests that, instead, she wants an all-out verbal fight—be aware that real communication will be impossible until you have allowed her to get over her anger or defensiveness. If someone responds to your initial statement about a problem in your relationship with arms crossed, eyes narrowed or fixed on yours, or body hunched backward, it may even be wise to retreat and reconsider what you should say. The individual is telling you via body language, "I don't care. My mind is closed to your ideas. No matter what you say, I'm not listening."

Sometimes talking can make things worse. Body language can be a clue that this isn't the time to get together with the person to address the problem. Consider scheduling a meeting at a later time when the person has had time to calm down.

Other signs to look for are clenched hands and fingers wrapped around an arm.

If you still want to address the problem there and then, adjust your body posture to suggest you are open to the person's remarks. One trick to begin to close the gap between this person and you: Begin to breathe at the same speed as the other person. This technique has been found to have a calming effect on someone who is upset. Mirroring the other's positive gestures may also do this.

As the person speaks, watch their gestures as well as actively listen to their words. You can gain insights into the issues of most importance by their body language.

Active Listening

Too often people are so involved with their own thoughts and desires that they devote 90 percent of their energy to sending messages and only 10 percent to hearing the other party. Some people are so involved in preparing what they will say next that they don't even hear the other party. Worse, some people hear through a filter of their own values and beliefs, and consequently fail to hear what is actually being said.

This is what often triggers the anger that precedes a conflict.

Active listening entails hearing someone out without intent of making an immediate judgment. It also means that we don't filter what we hear through our own viewpoint. Under such circumstances, disagreement is likely to escalate into arguments and ultimately a conflict. If you were to actively listen, you might be surprised to discover that there is no serious difference in opinion between you.

If you are practicing active listening, you should be able to answer "yes" to each of these questions:

- **Do you make eye contact with the person with whom you are speaking?** Give the person your full attention. By looking at a person's eyes, you are telling him that you are listening.

- **Do you nod your head and use appropriate facial expressions?** Nodding your head and facial gestures in sync with the person's words tell the speaker that you are hearing what he is saying.

- **Do you avoid distraction?** You don't want to suggest that your mind isn't on the discussion right here and now. When speaking to another, whatever the intent, don't look at your watch, shuffle papers, or otherwise suggest you are bored or disinterested in what the indivdiual has to say.

- **Do you ask questions?** Doing so not only tells the speaker that her comments interest you but help to clarify and ensure understanding.

- **Do you paraphrase?** Paraphrasing means restating what the other person has said in your own words. You paraphrase for two reasons. First, it's an excellent way to make sure that you listen; your mind can't wander if you know that you will have to paraphrase. Second, by saying in your own words what you think you heard from the speaker, you verify the accuracy of your understanding.

- **Do you interrupt?** Interrupting someone who is speaking is wrong at any time, and it can escalate an argument. Let the other person finish his thoughts before you respond. If the comments were heated, pause to allow yourself time to cool off just in case the remarks have angered you.

- **Do you move easily from role of listener to speaker?** There should be a smooth transition from one to the other and back again if you are listening to what the other person is saying. If you aren't, and are instead thinking about what you plan to say as soon as she finishes, the conversation will be uneven and unfocused.

Keep in mind that it's important in conflict management not only that the other person hear what you are saying but that you hear what he is saying. Many conflicts have several triggers, and if you listen carefully you may be able to identify each and every one of these. You, then, are in a position to address these issues. You won't have a long-lasting truce if you don't deal with *all* the causes of your problem with a colleague or manager.

Consequently, when you speak with someone with whom you are having problems, and the individual comes back at you in an argumentative manner, don't lose your cool and return in kind. Rather, listen carefully to the multiple issues being raised by the individual. After you've heard the individual out, allow for a moment of silence. Then in an even tone, ask the other person about the deeper-set issues you discerned from actively listening to the person's comments: "I wonder if you are upset about this project because you had hoped to chair it yourself?" Or, if you aren't sure about the other reasons but suspect they are there, you might say, "It seems that there may be other issues bothering you besides my request that you complete your assignment for the X project by the end of this week?" Such an observation, quietly stated, may open the door to further discussion. If the person denies the existence of other problems between you, despite your belief otherwise, focus on the problem at hand; don't press. If the place and time aren't suitable for discussion of the issue, then suggest meeting later in a non-threatening place to discuss the situation.

If the person admits to other reasons for being angry with you, then you both need more time to discuss the situation. Ask the individual if you can get together later in the day in a quiet environment, without distractions, where you can talk about the problem you both are having.

When Sandy found herself at odds with Laura about how to work with a vendor in installing a new computer network, Sandy suggested that Laura meet with her in the office cafeteria at 2:00 o'clock, when it was usually deserted, to discuss why Laura had e-mailed all computer users her recommendations without first consulting with Sandy. When Laura arrived, Sandy decided to probe beyond this situation to determine the hidden problems in their relationship. "Laura," she said, "you and I seem to be having some problems working together on this project. I want to work something out with you so that we're both comfortable working together."

At first, Laura was silent. Sandy was tempted to add more to her comment but, instead, chose to keep silent in the hope that it would prompt Laura to speak up, which it did.

"I know enough about the project," she said, "to have been given sole charge. I saw no reason for your involvement when we were both appointed to the task, and I see no involvement for you now," Laura said. Sandy recognized Laura's comment as a criticism of her abilities, but she held back a negative emotional reaction because it would only inflame Laura. Rather, she gently probed to determine why Laura felt as she did.

It turned out that Laura had worked in another firm and had overseen an installation very similar to that at Laura's and Sandy's company. As Sandy practiced active listening, she could sense that Laura, relatively new to the firm, had hoped that her sole appointment to the project would have earned her the attention of senior management. Very ambitious, Laura had taken the assistant's position as a step toward a staff position in systems, and she was impatient for the advancement she felt she deserved.

Sandy was equally ambitious but her goals had little to do with systems. She was interested in the systems' applications and particularly in the marketing department which she hoped one day to be in charge of. Sandy knew that Laura lacked knowledge about the organization, whereas Sandy knew little about the technology. She pointed this out to Laura, even went so far to assure her that she probably would have been made sole contact person had she been with the organization longer.

Once Sandy had identified the source of the problem with Laura, she and Laura discussed their individual goals and identified several possible solutions. They evaluated the pros and cons of each, and ultimately came up with a workable answer. Laura would work with the systems department and the vendor during the installation of the system; during this stage, Sandy would meet regularly with user departments to keep them informed of progress and identify all likely usages of the new system. The final report on the effort would come from Sandy and Laura but interim reports would come from Sandy or Laura depending on nature of the work, although there would be continuous communications and collaboration between the two.

As a final step, the two assistants developed a list of specific action steps for each and some rules to follow to ensure that neither sent out a report to management without first showing the report to the other.

Not all sessions will go so smoothly as this. In some situations, the best you can achieve with another person may be to agree to disagree. In many instances this may be due more to a personality conflict or a real problem other than miscommunication.

5

Personality Conflicts

Each and everyone of us has at least one person at work with whom we always seem to be at odds. How about you? Is there one person with whom you seldom get along well? It's particularly frustrating when we see that our view of this person isn't shared by others. This person snaps at us, or says something unnecessarily biting to us about our work or personal life, or otherwise makes us uncomfortable in their presence. Yet, if it's a co-worker, we see this person taking breaks with others and being asked by colleagues to join them for lunch. If it's a manager, our co-workers congratulate us about our good fortune to work for this person and say that they can't believe our stories about how terrible it is to work for this person.

Why is it that we are the only person who has trouble with this individual? Whose fault is it? What can we do to put an end to the conflict? And putting an end to the conflict is important, since the situation, besides being personally stressful to us, can influence our ability to work cooperatively with this individual—it can even affect our career with the firm.

Joe's Boss and Eileen's "Friend"

Joe likes his job and works hard. All of Joe's friends believe that he is an asset to the firm. What about Joe's boss, Mark? No one knows for sure. It's not that Mark has ever said anything negative about Joe's performance, but now and then he will make some comment to Joe, usually when they are alone, that is very hypercritical of Joe's work. These once-in-a-blue-moon comments, in Joe's opinion, are more representative of Mark's opinion of his work than any of the positive comments he writes in Joe's appraisals. And the likelihood of being zapped by Mark makes it uncomfortable for Joe to talk about work with him.

Everyone tells Joe to ignore Mark, because Mark has never taken any action to suggest he truly thinks Joe isn't carrying his weight. Mark just doesn't know how to express himself well, Joe's friends tell him.

Lenny, who also works in Mark's department, and has known Mark much longer than Joe, once told Joe, "Mark tries to be funny, but his idea of what's funny is . . . well . . . it's just off the mark," Lenny had said, laughing at his own pun.

But Joe wasn't amused. "Funny, huh," he had responded. "It's not funny when you've worked late the night before to help a customer, you step away from your desk for a minute to get a cup of coffee, and you find your boss waiting for you. He looks at the coffee and then says, 'I'm glad you got coffee. I'd hate management to walk by and see you with your head down snoring away.' He knew I put in a long night on the Zender account."

Is there something behind Mark's barbs? Or are Mark and Joe just so different that each unintentionally is rubbing the other the wrong way?

Here's another example of two people who can't seem to get along: Eileen and Lydia, administrative assistant to the sales vice president and executive secretary of the firm's CEO, respectively.

Eileen is a conscientious worker, always willing to help out when the need arises. When her boss asked her to come with him to a sales meeting in San Francisco and take charge of spouses during the three-day meeting, even put together a little event for them, she agreed willingly. It made sense to her: Her boss's wife usually took care of spouses during the annual meeting, but she had recently had a very serious operation. She was unable to handle the event, so Eileen's boss needed her to do it in his wife's place.

Eileen is respected by her peers, so it came as a surprise that there were whisperings about her going to San Francisco with her boss. "After all, she's attractive, and they'll be alone for three whole days," the rumor mill ground out. Eileen was shocked when she learned what was on the grapevine; however, she knew who was behind the rumor: Lydia. Not that Lydia would want to go to San Francisco and host the event, Eileen realized. She just seemed to envy anything that Eileen had. Ever since Eileen had been with the firm, Lydia had gone out of her way to say and do things to make Eileen's job difficult. It seemed to have started when Eileen joined a team that Lydia was running. Lydia had planned a very in-depth but unfocused approach to the project and Eileen had convinced the group to take a more linear approach to the project.

What is happening in these situations?

What's behind the ill will from Mark to Joe and similar response from Lydia to Eileen? To determine the answers to these questions, you need to know more about Mark, Joe, Eileen, and Lydia. How do they compare with the various personalities you are likely to encounter?

A Guide to Office Personalities

- **Mr. or Ms. Self-Confidence.** This individual has tremendous self-confidence. There's nothing that this person feels she is unable to accomplish. She'll take on new responsibilities and share ideas with anyone who gives her the opportunity to speak up. But she can come on very strong. When Ms. Self-Confidence lets herself go, she can trigger envy in some who would like to have the same confident nature, alienate others who worry about her taking over their turf, or intimidate those who believe they may be expected to accomplish as much as Ms. Self-Confidence.

- **The Party Person.** This person is very good at the job, but work often seems more like the backdrop for this person. He prefers joking with friends and keeping track of their families and personal lives. High on life, this person always seems ready to celebrate some happening in the office, which can make those who are more focused on their work, who may even carry the adjective "workaholic," feel unsociable and out of it.

- **The Busy Bee.** This could be our workaholic. She may or may not possess the same level of self-confidence as Ms. Self-Confidence, but she certainly doesn't get the same level of recognition—she doesn't know how to sell herself or her ideas. She's not a party person, since she believes that she's at the office to work, not to socialize. The busy bee is often overlooked by others in the organization—not only managers but her peers. When you step on the busy bee inadvertently, you need to know that this person can sting, even if it's only to make your job tougher. Many bureaucratic types are busy bees.

- **The Contradictor.** This person will disagree just to get attention. Irascible, he can be difficult to work with, particularly if you hold strong views on an issue yourself. Even if you compromise your own opinion and agree with this person in order to make peace, you may find yourself still at war with this person. The contradictor likes to fight so much that he'll change positions just to keep battling. The only way you may be able to get this individual to cooperate is if you insist that he justify his objections.

- **The Nervous Wretch.** This individual seems to take pleasure in worrying about anything and everything. Very different from Mr. or Ms. Self-Confidence, this person worries not only about assuming new tasks but even his day-to-day work. If you work with the nervous wretch, you may never get assignments on time—your peer will be double- and triple-checking the work to be sure he hasn't made any mistakes.

- **The Analytical Type.** This person likes to look at all aspects of a situation. If she's your boss, or she's a peer on a project team with you, you'll find that her desire to be sure about what is happening will test your patience.

- **The Autocrat.** This individual is a perfectionist, unwilling to tolerate errors. If he's a manager, don't expect him to delegate anything to you. Whether boss or peer, don't expect to get information from this individual. Information is power and the autocrat will hoard what he knows. If you have a co-worker like this, and you have to work together, you will find him attempting to dominate you. And your resistance will prevent a harmonial relationship from developing.

  If the autocrat is your boss, you'll feel thwarted unless you are a busy bee quite content to do your job quietly in a corner of the hive.

- **The Buddy.** This person exudes warmth and friendliness. She's quite congenial but she'll tell you what she thinks you want to hear—you'll never get a straight answer. It's more important for this person to be your friend than to do a job right.

If you have a co-worker on your staff who is always visiting you and others, seems a little disorganized about her work, and is very casual about important details, your co-worker is likely a buddy.

- **The Politician.** You won't get an answer to a question. Rather, you'll get the question, "What do you think we should do?" This person seems willing to listen to suggestions and tends to look at the big picture. On the negative side, however, she doesn't appreciate the work involved in reaching the big picture and she'll often take credit for your ideas. Manipulative, this person will always be looking for ways around the rules and quick and easy ways to impress others.

  If you are conscientious, straightforward in your opinions, and creative (but desirous of getting credit for your ideas), you won't get along well with the politician. The politician may see you as a threat if your boss and co-workers are aware of your talents.

These personality types are only some of those you will find in your organization. Look around to see if can identify others based on your job experiences. Consider your own qualities, too. Would you fit in one of the categories I've listed, or another? Are you even-tempered or do you blow up easily? Are you open-minded about others' ideas or insistent on your ideas? Are you a rule breaker or rule bender or rule follower? All these qualities and others will influence your relationship with others and the likelihood of personality conflicts with them.

Forcing two people who are very similar to work together can lead to dissonance. But so can forcing two individuals who are very, very different.

Let's look at Joe and Mark and Eileen and Lydia.

Those who know Mark well would label him an autocrat. Yes, he's fair about his employees' performance, but he's always on the alert for evidence that someone isn't pulling their weight. Joe, on the other hand, is a socializer. Yes, he's a hard worker but he also likes to work because of the enjoyment in working with people he likes. Mark sees Joe socializing with friends at his desk, and he worries that Joe isn't focused on the work. He doesn't have any reason to doubt Joe's performance, but that hasn't prevented him from being concerned, so he drops an occasional dig to remind Joe about the importance of the work.

Lydia is an unrecognized busy bee whereas Eileen is a self-confident who has won accolades for her accomplishments. Lydia is always looking for faults in Eileen because these weaknesses make Lydia feel superior.

In both cases, the potential for conflict stems from the differences in personality. But other problems would arise if they were very similar in personality. If Mark and Joe were both socializers, no work would get done—they would spend the workday talking. If they were both auto-crats, there would be a power struggle between the two. If Lydia were a self-confident like Eileen, she might be so eager to demonstrate her ability that she might try to hold Eileen down. If Eileen were a busy bee like Lydia, she and Lydia might get along better, but it would be a detri-ment to Eileen's advancement.

What's Behind the Differences?

It's fun to give names like "the busy bee" or "the workaholic" to differ-ent people, but what is really the difference? And, more important, what can you do to minimize problems in working with someone who is either too different or too much like you?

If you think of people in terms of personality style, they actually fall into four categories:

- **Task-oriented.** One person who falls into this category is "The Analytical" in that she wants the facts and looks for background information and other data before taking action on something. An-alyticals are knowledgeable about their work, and enjoy the reputa-tion as experts in their field, capable of preventing or solving problems in their area of expertise. Another group of task-oriented people are autocrats. "Busy bees" are also task-oriented. Lydia, for instance, relies on lots of to-do lists to ensure her efficiency, and she is very focused on her work. For her, it's important to be considered productive. She likes a work challenge and is proud of her loyalty to her job—sometimes, she sacrifices her own self-interest and the needs of her family in the name of loyalty to her work.

Another analytical group: the worry wretch. These people are forever looking for proof that the work was done correctly.

- **The Socializer.** Joe is a socializer, warm, friendly, helpful, and caring of his colleagues. Affiliation-oriented, he wants to be part of the group, and he resents anyone or anything that makes him feel like he's an outsider. Mark's comments, whatever their reason, make Joe feel as if Mark is questioning Joe's support of the group, and that, and less its implications to his career, upsets him. That's why it is so important that Joe meet daily over lunch with his pals to talk about the work he is doing and the events in his department and friends' work areas.

Joe dislikes change because it could threaten his affiliation with the company and his relationships there. So when several major and minor rules were implemented last year by Mark, and many procedures and policies dramatically changed, Joe was more upset about schedule changes that meant that he could no longer lunch at 1 p.m. with his pals, than he was about the negative impact some of the new policies had on his ability to immediately solve customers' concerns.

Other socializers: the party person and the buddy.

- **Visionary.** This is someone who is a leader or a potential leader, continually pushing the envelope either with respect to the work or to his or her performance. Yes, Eileen has lots of visionary in her. She's interested in learning and doing more and ultimately moving up in the organization. For her, a challenge would be to be put in charge of a team and be given the opportunity to accomplish something important (in her opinion) to the organization. She likes it when she is complimented for her professional image and her foresight and creativity. She has lots of friends in the organization, and she is as efficient as Lydia, but her major motivation is the desire for some power to make a difference.

There is a negative side to many visionaries: Some have grand schemes but give little thought to implementation of these ideas.

They make assumptions without verifying them, and they depend on others to put their ideas to work without providing the resources for them to make it so.

The politician is a visionary in that she wants more power. On the other hand, this person often uses affiliations rather than skills and knowledge about the organization, or willingness to extend herself, to gain that power. Depending on her personality and the organization's culture, the politician may also utilize broad concepts and business buzzwords without a clear action plan or understanding of the implications.

- **Conceptualizer.** These individuals tend to see the big picture, and they often need others to fill in the details. The conceptualizer can take many forms, from a contradictor if he expects to be consulted for every decision to implement the grand plan (regardless of the efficiency of doing so), to an autocrat, unwilling to risk errors and insistent that everything be done as she demands, to a nervous wretch, who hovers over those to whom was delegated the implementation of the abstract concept or idea.

At this point, you may be thinking about those with whom you work to see if you recognize their personality types. Keep in mind, however, that it isn't just the negative side of each of these personalities that is behind any conflicts you have with them. Conflict stems from an interaction between two or more people, and to identify the nature of a conflict you have to consider your own personality's effect on the person or persons with whom you have the conflict, as well as the effect of the other persons' personality or style on you.

Besides analyzing your boss or a co-worker with whom you are having troubles, you need to think about where in these four categories you fall. You may see some of yourself in each category, but try to determine your predominant style. To help, here are some "yes" or "no" questions to ask yourself:

- I'm known for being cooperative.
- I leave the specific plans to others.
- I dislike working alone.
- I like to prioritize my work and work according to my plan.

- I enjoy being a part of a group.
- I will bring my work home to get it done.
- I am not comfortable in periods of change.
- I am always ready to assume more responsibility.
- I prefer to leave the details to others.
- I think I don't have enough authority.
- I like to prevent or solve problems.
- I am very critical of others.
- I'm known as someone who will bend the rules to reach my goal.
- I believe in following the rules.

Are you primarily an analytical, a visionary, a conceptualizer, or a socializer?

Now, using the same questions, ask yourself about that person with whom you continually have trouble: Does the person have a reputation for being difficult to work with? Does she prefer to leave the details to others? Does the person think he doesn't have enough authority? Consider each question in terms of the person with whom you have problems. Based on the answers to these questions, where would you place this person among the four categories? Not only will this process give you insights into how to work more productively with the other person, but it should also give you insights into how to minimize the likelihood of future conflicts between you and the person. [Parenthetically, the same process should be done each time you have to work with some new person. A better understanding of the individual's personality style will make it easier for you to understand the person and work with him. You may even want to adapt your style to the other person's to prevent disagreement and work cooperatively.]

Let's assume that you are a visionary but your boss is a conceptualizer. You may want to learn to speak your boss's language in sharing your vision or ideas with her. You may also want to encourage your boss to empower you to implement your mutual goal. Since neither of you brings task orientation to the equation, you may have to assume that responsibility, helping your boss see how she can make the abstract idea workable.

Let's look at another combination. Let's say that you are an analytical and your co-worker is a socializer. You have found it difficult to get your colleague's support to complete a project. You might want to use pressure, pointing out how your other co-workers need your work done to do their own work. Or you might want to build a rapport with the other person, spending a lunchtime in small talk before you get down to work, or involve mutual friends in the work to get the individual's full support.

What if you are an analytical and your boss is predominately a visionary? You may want to sit down every week to review the goals for the week, getting agreement from your boss on how each goal will be reached by setting up action plans in concert. Where you expect to encounter problems, raise the issues and identify solutions. Use your meeting time to develop contingency plans to ensure you are able to stretch the envelope as your boss wishes.

Answers to Personality Conflicts

Admittedly, personality conflicts have always existed and will continue to exist. You can't expect to get along together in an amiable way with everyone in your organization, but there are things you can do to lessen the tension in a personality conflict. They won't guarantee 100-percent the end of the conflict but they should make your work situation more peaceful:

- **Be self-introspective.** Each time a conflict arises you need to ask this very important question: How am I contributing to the personality conflict? For instance, an office professional who is always in a hurry may frustrate and even alienate another who needs time to question her manager about some work that needs to be done. Or an employee with an untidy work station may be perceived by you, an analytical, as disorderly, but in reality this person may be a visionary and top performer. Learn to ignore the messy desk and focus on the person's sharp mind.
- **Accentuate the positive.** If the individual is making an effort to work cooperatively with you, despite differences in outlook, demonstrate your appreciation of the effort. If it's your boss, let her know that you welcome her effort.

- **Talk with the individual.** A frequently overlooked tactic is to talk to the person in a mature fashion. Talk in a frank but nonthreatening manner, as described in Chapter 4.
- **Keep communication channels open.** You can only do further harm to your relationship with a manager or co-worker by cutting off communication, even if it is only about work.
- **Treat everyone alike.** If you are a supervisor and your conflict is with someone who reports to you, don't single this person out for any better or worse treatment than other employees. If the conflict is with a peer, be as cooperative with this individual as other colleagues.
- **Agree to disagree.** If all else fails, you may want to meet with the individual to agree that you have innate differences but that you will put these aside and work together. Just as talking out the problem may reveal that your boss doesn't know that her behavior is making you uncomfortable, or that you don't know something you are doing bothers a colleague, agreeing to disagree may likewise get you past the personality conflict. In focusing on work, you and your boss or co-worker may, in time, create a productive partnership that overrides any personality differences.

6

Getting to the Problem

Some conflicts aren't due to poor communications or personality differences but to operating weaknesses. The angry words and hard feelings are responses to wrestling with the problem. In such instances, to resolve the conflict, you have to identify the nature of the problem and solve it either on your own or with the help of the other party, or the hard feelings remain.

The conflict resolution advice in the first section of this book won't eliminate permanently the conflict unless the underlying problem is addressed. Otherwise, either the hard feelings remain, making a cooperative work effort impossible, or the conflict is buried but able to resurface over the very next issue.

What kinds of problems or issues are we talking about? Any and all kinds for which one result may be feelings of anger directed toward one person or group. This means they can involve anyone from a janitor to a CEO and could include office professionals, bosses, or customers, or any combination thereof. The problem doesn't have to be complex, like a manufacturing snafu, poor product design, or budget battle, although any of these can lead ultimately to conflict. Actually, the simpler the complaint, the more likely its cause won't be addressed, although the subsequent emotional reaction may remain. Such conflicts can arise, for instance, when someone is being given more work or only the least interesting work, whereas others have smaller workloads or more interesting assignments; a person's performance is being assessed by a boss unfamiliar with the person's work; unclear instructions cause someone to stay late frequently; indecisiveness means work has to be redone and then redone again; or, as with Kate and Francine, information that is regularly needed to do a task is never provided on time.

The Case of Kate and Francine

Kate is administrative assistant to Doug, senior vice president in charge of operations for a midwestern manufacturing firm. Francine holds a similar position with the head of production, Steve, one of Doug's managers. Every second Thursday, Steve has to provide Doug with an operating report that Doug, in turn, uses to make a presentation for the planning group Friday afternoon. To prepare his report, Steve needs information on raw materials purchases during the previous two weeks. This information is available in a report prepared for Doug by purchasing, another area that is under his direction. Purchasing's data are processed on Wednesday, and its report is printed that day, but the final document isn't distributed until Friday, even to Doug.

Francine didn't know this. She assumed that purchasing's report went out either late Wednesday or early Thursday. When Steve didn't get his copy by noon on Thursday, she would call Kate for the information she and her boss needed to do the report for Doug. Because she thought that his failure to get the report was due to his name not being on the distribution list, she also would ask Kate to check to see if Steve was listed to get a copy. Kate would reassure her that Steve was on the list, but Francine had her doubts: Why, then, didn't he get his copy on Thursday, after the reports were printed? Why did he get it on Friday, right after she called Kate?

Francine thought that Kate had sent it from Doug's office after being reminded that Steve needed a copy of the report.

What began as a small nuisance became a major irritant—to both Francine and Kate. Francine believed that Kate was indifferent to the problem because, as assistant to the operations vice-president, she felt herself above the other assistants. Due to Kate's regal bearing, she began to refer to Kate as "Queen Kate" and the nickname stuck and other assistants began to use the name behind Kate's back.

Because Kate didn't realize that Steve and Francine needed one bit of information on the report to produce their own biweekly report, she thought Francine should learn some patience. She had been assured by purchasing that Steve's name was on the distribution list and that he was receiving the report at the same time that all the managers who reported to Doug got it—every second Friday.

Francine's and Kate's irritation led to heated words when Kate asked Francine to send her brochures on new office technology, which she needed to make a case for upgrading her work station. Kate called Francine on Monday, but she still hadn't received the material by Wednesday. She decided to stop by Francine's desk to pick up the material. As she walked in, she heard Francine telling some co-workers how she deliberately was holding on to the material to teach Kate a lesson. "This will teach Queen Kate what it feels like to ask regularly for something from someone and get no cooperation," she said.

"Be careful," said Genie, another office professional. "Queen Kate might order you decapitated." "Yeah," said Margaret, another member of the group, "It could be 'off with your head'."

The three assistants looked up and saw Kate. Kate was deeply hurt by what she had heard but she also was angry. "How dare you?" she asked, adding some descriptive nouns to her query that the three office professionals were shocked to discover Kate knew. "You denigrate me although I stop what I'm doing to help you when you need information from purchasing," she said. "Next time you need help from purchasing, you can call one of your pals in the department."

She then marched out of the work area.

"Oh, boy," said Margaret. "I've never seen Kate this angry."

"I wonder what she meant about purchasing," said Francine, reaching for the phone to call Geri, the assistant to the head of purchasing.

That's when Francine learned that Kate had regularly called Geri for purchasing's raw materials figures for her. "But why?" Francine asked. "I don't know," Geri answered. "If she waited a day, she would have the information herself."

"What?" said Francine. Geri then explained how purchasing's reports were distributed on Friday. "Your boss is one of those who gets a copy,"

Geri added. "Kate had me double-check a few weeks back; I looked at the distribution list, and his name was on it," she continued. "You do get it every second Friday, don't you?" she asked, confused.

"Yes," said Francine, acknowledging that Steve did, indeed, get a copy of the report the day it was distributed. She knew she was going to have to eat crow. So, calling Kate, Francine apologized for her disrespectful behavior.

Kate's royal bearing was only a disguise to hide her warm heart, and she accepted the apology graciously. But the conversation didn't end there. Both office professionals realized that there was a problem in the distribution of division reports. People were getting reports too late to do them any good. There had to be some better order of distribution. Kate and Francine decided to talk to their respective bosses to get them to investigate the matter. Doug and Steve agreed that they had a problem and they charged Kate and Francine with the task of finding a workable solution, which they did.

Had they not, and had the reporting problem continued, in time the angry feelings might have resurfaced, although this time Kate, Francine, and maybe Steve would be together on one side of the conflict and Doug, Geri, her boss, and perhaps the head of purchasing on the other side.

In this instance, the situation involved two office professionals. But problems involving an office professional and her boss, an office professional and a staff member, or two bosses can exist that, left unsolved, can develop into a conflict. Let me share another story; this one involves an office professional and her boss. Whereas Kate and Francine work in a large multinational firm, this story takes place in a one-manager office.

The Case of Linda and Murray

Linda is an office professional. Her boss is owner of a theatrical agency in Beverly Hills. Besides handling media contacts for his clients, he's their business manager.

Because Murray gets so many calls from reporters to interview his clients, he has Linda screen his calls; if he dealt with all the requests personally, he wouldn't have time to handle his clients' financial needs. But fielding all the incoming calls means that Linda has less time herself to support Murray with this other side of the agency, a situation which Linda thought that Murray understood, until she was called into Murray's office to discuss several undone tasks.

Murray pointed to a stack of letters yet to be mailed—Murray has yet to enter the computer age, so he either dictates letters, writes them in longhand for Linda, or scribbles notes for Linda in order for her to ghost letters for him—a contract with a new performer to be completed, stacks of papers to be filed, and clippings about his clients that need to be copied and the copies sent to the celebrities.

Linda heard Murray out and then let loose with her own litany of complaints about Murray, including his indecisiveness, nitpicking about the letters she wrote under his name, poor penmanship, and his failure to keep her informed about where he was going when he left the office, something that increasingly was putting her in an awkward spot when either a client or reporter called to speak to him.

The two then went to their separate corners—he to his private office, and she to her desk in the outer office. At the end of the day, Murray left with a curt "Good night" and Linda was left with a stack of paperwork to get done. One of Murray's biggest clients was doing a singing tour through Europe, and she had had call after call to handle, so she had been unable to get to the paperwork once again.

As her eyes moved to her computer screen, she also saw at least 20 messages from lifestyle magazines and other periodicals that covered TV, movies, and the stage that would require response. "He thinks the computer has made my job easier," she thought. "He has no appreciation of my job," Linda thought. Before she began the work, Linda decided to call her husband to let him know that she would be home late again. As she was bemoaning her situation, he stopped her. Mike said, "Linda, come on, you like the curmudgeon. You've had to stay late a few times in the past but never like this; it's due to the tour and Murray's new clients. Think about it, hon. Put your mind to the problem, and see what you and Murray can do to sort things out."

As Linda listened, she realized her husband was right. She liked her job, and she even liked Murray—he gave her lots of authority and she was fairly paid for everything she did for him. The next day when Murray arrived, the stack of letters were still on his desk. So were the files and clippings. But there was another piece of paper. It was a proposal to address the firm's new and bigger workload. In her analysis, Linda pointed out how Murray's small theatrical firm had grown beyond the point that he and one assistant could manage—it was time to bring in some help for her.

She listed her responsibilities and the time it took to handle the media contacts, administrative work, and clerical support. She had called a temp-and-placement firm and had cost figures for a temp to help over the short term, during the current tour of the firm's big client, and potential salary for a full-time assistant for her if Murray agreed with her that the problem would likely continue and even grow.

The plan also included the consequences of not pursuing her plan: Murray would have to take over media contacts in order to free her to handle the administrative *and* clerical support work.

Murray read the document and then called Linda into the office. They both apologized to the other, each blaming the hectic pace from the added workload for the exchange the afternoon before. The two then looked at the costs of bringing help into the office. Murray argued that the firm couldn't afford a full-time assistant for Linda but he did agree to a temp, three days a week, to handle clerical support. He also promised to review the situation with her in six months to see if a temp was still sufficient to allow her to continue her current responsibilities without falling behind in her administrative work.

In both cases above, the parties were fortunate that circumstances helped them to see beyond the conflict to the existence of a problem. It enabled them to separate personal feelings from the problem and address it. I can't say that Kate and Francine became bosom buddies after resolving the report distribution problem, but I can say that there was one less reason for a conflict arising between them that would make it impossible for them to work cooperatively. And resolving the problem set a pattern of communication for them that reduced the likelihood of future conflicts—likewise, Linda and Murray.

Murray is guilty of all that Linda accused him of, but he is also a fair boss who is appreciative of the work that Linda does. She did get her

assistant six months later, but it demanded that she and Murray im-
prove the communications between them. In fact, telling me this story,
Linda admitted that the real cause of the explosion that day between
Murray and her wasn't the issue of staff but rather her failure to keep
Murray abreast of the number of incoming calls from the press and its
impact on her workload.

Problem Solving

Is there a way to tell if a conflict between you and another person is due
to a communication misunderstanding, personality conflict, or a real
issue? Yes, there is, but it isn't easy. It requires that you suppress any
emotional reaction to a situation and delve for its cause. Ask questions
rather than let yourself respond emotionally, which you may be
prompted to do if the other's words are heated.

You shouldn't immediately dismiss a complaint, interrupt, defend your
position or another's, or otherwise respond from an emotional bias that
you are right and the other person is wrong. Before you can make a
judgment about the cause behind a conflict that has arisen, you have to
do what you should do with any conflict: Listen to the issues and determine the facts that will affect your response.

Communication Basics

Let's consider what happened between Kate and Francine again. The
situation could have been remedied much sooner if Francine had
thought to ask Kate why she repeatedly had to call for the information
her boss needed. Likewise, Kate could have asked Francine why she
didn't call purchasing directly for the information or why she couldn't
wait until the next day when the report from purchasing was distributed. Instead, both assistants reacted emotionally to the situation, seeing the behavior of the other as affronts to their positions or as
disregard of their needs. The secret to determining if a real problem is
behind a conflict involves four steps:

1. **Focus on the issue, not the person.** If need be, let the other party
   vent his frustration or anger before you try to identify the real issue
   behind the conflict. But hold in your own desire to get your say in.

For instance, Linda felt the need to get in her two cents' worth after hearing out Murray, but it could only have escalated the conflict if Murray wasn't a mensch.

2. **Listen to the issues.** Linda would have been wiser had she heard Murray out and then pointed out the impact that his new clients' work was having on her workload. At the very least, he would have better understood the situation. Even better, they might have solved the problem together—and with Murray's buy-in earlier, she might have had her full-time assistant sooner.

3. **Center the discussion on fixing the problem, not placing blame.** This is what Linda was able to do ultimately. She could have spent her overtime blaming Murray for having to stay late night after night, or she could—as she did—examine the nature of the problem and come up with a solution that would satisfy her needs and his.

4. **Get all the facts.** Critical to preventing a conflict from going underground, only to arise again, which an unsolved problem will do when you treat the symptom rather than the real cause, is to understand the full nature of the situation. In some instances, you may have to talk not only to the person with whom you are in conflict but to others who can offer their viewpoints to help you put the problem into perspective.

Sarah's Dilemma

So far we have discussed simple problems. But what do you do with more complex problems? Consider what happened to Sarah.

Her company had reorganized, and Sarah found herself with four bosses rather than three. Besides three marketing managers, Sarah also reported to Deidre, the head of customer service. Plus Sarah got some new responsibilities.

The organization installed new data collection systems, and the marketing managers found they could do more targeted marketing if they received weekly customer information. Each of the three assigned both data inputting and analysis to Sarah.

Ray, one of the three marketing managers, wasn't unrealistic; he recognized that Sarah's workload had grown significantly, and he arranged for her to have an assistant. Unfortunately, Sarah's new assistant had a view of her job different from the job description and often made end-runs around Sarah to Ray, the senior marketing manager, and to Deidre. Sarah spoke to Lynette about the situation but Lynette was deaf to her complaint. Lynette would remind Sarah that she officially reported to Ray, and Ray wasn't concerned—actually, he liked having two people to pass his work to. So did Deidre. But the other two managers to whom Sarah reported were unhappy with the situation.

Sarah would pass on their tasks to Lynette, who left them for last, working on Deidre's and Ray's jobs first. In the end, Sarah had to do all the work for these two managers herself as well as Ray's market reports.

Sarah tried to teach Lynette how to enter the marketing data for the weekly market reports and conduct the analyses, but Lynette always had work to do for either Deidre or Ray. Consequently, she never learned how to handle that part of the department's work.

The situation came to a head when Sarah went on her vacation. On the day she returned, she discovered that none of the market reports had been done and the two marketing managers were barking at Ray because the reports as well as other work they had given Lynette to do hadn't been done. Worse, during her absence, Lynette had failed to follow up on a customer call about the status of his shipment and, upset about the lack of service, the customer had taken his account elsewhere. It was Ray's account and he blamed it on Deidre. They had had words in Deidre's office, and Deidre had been called to the office of the division vice-president about the incident.

As Sarah walked to her desk, everyone transferred the anger built over the previous 14 days to her. She could have allowed herself to get swept up in the turmoil in the office and pass the blame on to Lynette for everything that had gone wrong. But Sarah believed that the problem wasn't so simple, and she decided to wait until the work on her desk was cleared up before going to Deidre to discuss the situation. As the most senior person to whom she reported, she chose her as the person with whom to discuss the matter.

Sarah knew that Deidre could get the support of all three marketing managers, even Ray, to prevent the problem's recurrence. First, however, Deidre and Sarah had to agree on what had *really* happened.

Deidre admitted that she and Ray should have been tougher on Lynette, but she argued that Sarah was responsible for what had happened because she hadn't adequately trained Lynette. It wasn't easy for Sarah to hold her tongue, but she let Deidre speak her piece and did not interrupt. Only after Deidre had detailed all that had gone wrong in her absence did Sarah speak.

Yes, she said, Lynette should have been taught how to enter data and analyze the market reports but she often begged off, explaining that she was doing work for Ray or Deidre. Sarah reminded Deidre that she had spoken to both her and Ray about the situation but to no avail. In Lynette's defense, however, Sarah reminded Deidre that Lynette was being asked to handle the same heavy workload she and Sarah were both responsible for.

"All right," said Deidre, "it probably was unrealistic for us to expect her to input data, analyze and produce the market reports, and also do everyone's correspondence and clerical work." "But," she added, "she also lost us a key customer." Deidre then went on to explain how the client had called, had asked about the status of his order, but had not heard from Lynette although she had promised to get back to him with the information.

"I can appreciate the problem she would have with shipping," Sarah told Deidre. "We have no system there that keeps tabs on orders; it makes queries like that difficult to handle. I know people in shipping who are able to get back to me before the day is over with the information I need."

Deidre remembered that the company had postponed installing a warehouse data system because of the high cost of installing the other new systems. "I should talk to the division v-p," she told Sarah. "I'll talk to Ray about Lynette," she continued. "Since she is your assistant, she should report to you." In the meantime, she told Sarah, "teach Lynette how to input data and prepare those market reports. I don't want this kind of problem to recur next year."

"Next year, it won't," Sarah said. "When I go on vacation, I'm going to ask for a temp to help Lynette with clerical support. I think that's another thing that this situation has taught us," she reminded Deidre. "Yes, you're right," Deidre agreed.

While Sarah's words with Deidre didn't immediately do away with the glares she and Lynette received from Ray and the other two marketing managers, her controlled reaction prevented the escalation of hard feelings.

Five Additional Steps

Let's recap how Sarah handled the situation. She followed the four steps described above but she went further to get to the heart of the problem. Let's review these additional five steps:

5. **Define the problem.** This step is critical in problem solving—and with cause. If you don't define a problem correctly, you will wind up solving the wrong problem, which likely means that the original problem will reappear. On the surface, the problem here seemed to be only Sarah's failure to train Lynette properly. In reality, there were two more serious problems. First, during Sarah's vacation, Lynette was expected to do the work of two, which was unrealistic given not only the workload but Lynette's lack of knowledge about some of the responsibilities. Second, Lynette was expected to get information for a customer that even Sarah, a ten-year veteran with the firm, had a hard time getting when she handled such requests.

6. **Collect all information that seems relevant to the problem.** You want to know as much as possible about what happened. Which was why it was important for Sarah to hear Deidre out to find out all that had happened in her absence.

7. **Identify as many possible causes of the problem as you can.** There were several reasons for the problems that occurred during Sarah's absence, some more serious than others. Sarah had to identify each one if she was to prevent the situation's recurrence.

8. **Identify solutions for solving the problem(s).** Talking to those closest to the problem or who have an investment in the problem's solution is the simplest way to solving problems like this. But some problems may require more complex techniques, such as the use of analytical tools like Pareto or Gantt charts.

Brainstorm alone or with others to determine answers to the problem, which is what Deidre did with Sarah, her customer reps, the three marketing managers, and warehouse manager, to find a quick-fix for the lack of a warehouse report system until a computerized one could be installed.

9. **Implement your solution.** The plan would include an agenda along with specific steps to put the plan into action. In this instance, the plan included a change in reporting relationships, informal and formal training for Lynette, and development of a system to track customer orders.

"This is all well and good," you may say, "but how do I get an individual who is venting about a problem to undertake this process with me if the problem isn't readily visible, like the lack of an order-tracking system?" The secret in getting someone to go through the final five steps is the practice of the first four steps.

While you may want to give back what you are getting from the other party—if possible, to outshout or out-insult, or otherwise defend yourself—the only way to resolve conflicts is to stay silent until the other party is able to talk reasonably and sanely about the matter. Then, and only then, are you in a position to determine if the conflict is attributable to more than a personality conflict or miscommunication and is instead a byproduct of an operating issue or other problem that needs to be addressed.

Section III

Building Better Relationships

7

Boss/Office Professional Relationships

You have probably disagreed with your boss at one time or another. But the chance of conflicts in the workplace will be greater in the future, for two reasons.

First, managers are being asked to do much more in less time. This adds to the stress of the workplace and the likelihood of short tempers and angry words on your boss's part—and yours—as you support your boss in her work.

Second, conflicts between you and your boss may arise as you both adjust to your new partnership in which you have increased responsibility. It is a role that is not yet clearly defined. Which means that differences between you and your boss (about your tasks, decision-making authority, recognition, and rewards) are likely to occur.

In today's volatile workplace, there will be occasions when you and your boss won't "be on the same page." But the key to surviving these situations is to not let the situation get to you personally. Your goal should be to maintain a harmonious working relationship with your boss, even in moments of high stress or confusion about your authority.

You may even have a special boss problem with which to contend. Even in good times, your boss may be too controlling or too temperamental, too indecisive, or just disagreeable. In today's leaner organizations, it may even be impossible to work with such a boss without an occasional shouting match, initiated either by you or by him. If it's impossible, in your opinion, for you and your boss to have a healthy, harmonious working relationship most of the time, if not all, then it may be time to cut the cord and look elsewhere for a job.

Even then, you shouldn't use this occasion to express the frustrations you have kept under control during your work relationship. While you might want to give her a piece of your mind, better not burn your bridges. Identify something outstanding that your boss did during your association, and extend your appreciation. You never know when you might need a recommendation from an ex-boss who drove you to distraction but whom you left thinking well of you.

Conflict between you and your boss as you depart can damage your career prospects as much, if not more, than conflict while working for the individual. But let's take a more positive view. Here are suggestions designed to reduce the likelihood of conflicts, resolve any that occur, and build a stronger partnership between you and your boss.

The Matter of Disagreements

As mentioned earlier, conflict is a part of the human condition, and you and your boss, as human beings, are likely to view things in conflicting ways from time to time. When you don't see eye to eye:

- **Stick to the facts.** Don't argue based on opinion. Rather, base your case on numbers, events, or documents that can be closely and objectively studied. You may disagree with your boss's stand but don't cast aspersions on the accuracy of her assessment or take potshots at her thinking, because that can trigger harsh words. On the other hand, you should be prepared for your boss to question your facts or thinking, the degree of her doubt dependent upon not only the case you present but also on your boss's relationship with you and your own weaknesses.

  A poor relationship between you and your boss, or with an insecure boss (think "defensive" even), generally means harsher evaluation of your ideas.

- **Help your boss to reexamine the situation.** You want to engage in a dialogue, not a diatribe, with your boss to get him to rethink the logic behind his case. Ideally, you should both be willing to look at a situation from the other's vantage point. If you come on too strong, however, you can make your boss deaf to your side of the situation.

- **Don't try to antagonize your boss.** It may be frustrating to think that your side, idea, or view of a situation isn't being given a fair hearing, but you shouldn't verbalize your frustration in terms that antagonize, such as "unrealistic," "flawed," "mistaken," or "unfair."

    Such terms act like matches to a stack of dry kindling; if they don't ignite the kindling, they set the stage for a major conflagration in the future.

- **Know when to back off.** Keep in mind that you are talking to your boss, and you can go only so far trying to persuade her to accept your view. It doesn't matter the seriousness of the situation. You have to know when to give up.

    This applies even in the case of performance assessments. Let's say that you feel your boss's evaluation of your work is unfair. Your boss is not taking into consideration certain extenuating circumstances, such as lack of cooperation from others within the organization, confusion over the objectives to be achieved, or unrealistic expectations. You can take the issue over your boss's head to her supervisor or to human resources, but if neither action is successful, then you have no choice but to accept your boss's assessment and demonstrate over the next year its inaccuracy, or move on either within the organization or outside.

The Stressful Workplace

Bosses may be less patient in today's work climate, and you may be the brunt of this impatience. Your boss may seem to be continually demanding more and more from you in the way of work. Further, someone who previously *asked* may begin to *demand* or tell you to do something, and expect you to juggle multiple tasks with minimal complaints. It's a pressure-cooker environment, and that means that you need to find the right time, right place, and boss in the right mood to bring up any issues, not just complaints but also job tasks, ideas, and news you feel your boss has a need to know.

- **Don't interrupt your boss during a crisis period.** If you need to talk to your boss, find a time when your boss doesn't seem harried by all the work around him. You're less likely to get his attention or his approval if you choose a moment when your boss already feels too many demands upon him to ask, for instance, for a day off. You'll be upset either by the answer you get or tone in which your request is handled, and your boss will be upset if it distracts him from work.

Donna is an administrative assistant for the chief financial officer. She always seemed to need her boss when he was on his way to or from the CEO's office with some major project that needed to be done in the next 60 minutes. Rather than stop and talk to her, Peter would race by, on one occasion almost knocking her out of his way. Donna tried to be understanding but over time Peter's indifference to the pressures his work put on her began to get to her. Nor did she keep her feelings inside. Peter became the target of blatant hints (think "rude") about his behavior; with too much to do already, Peter had no desire to deal with an irritated secretary as well. So, to prevent a confrontation, he would take the long way around to the CEO's office. Immediately after a meeting, if he had a rush task, he would lock his door so even Donna wouldn't be able to get in.

The situation would have continued indefinitely, but one evening Donna overheard him on the phone as she was getting her coat to leave for the day. He was telling a colleague just how busy he was and how irritating it was to have to tiptoe around his assistant since she seemed to have no idea about the amount of work he had to get done. "Does he think I don't appreciate his responsibilities?" Donna thought. "I'm well aware of the many demands on his time; I'm the one who is forever being asked to get some answer from him because he's not available to a staff member or manager." Donna decided there and then to discuss the problem with Peter.

The next morning when Peter entered the office, he found on his computer calendar an appointment with Ms. Troy for 8:30 a.m. As he looked up, Donna Troy walked into his office, with two cups of coffee and some danishes in a cakebox. "I feel there is a problem between us," she told him. "I overheard you yesterday evening, and . . . ." He started to interrupt but she continued. "I think you are very busy, but so am I. I am continually dealing with the demands of colleagues who want a few minutes of your time or some report or other thing from you.

I believe that we need to find time to address these issues, or a way to handle them without distracting you from your work."

Peter was speechless. When he thought about it, he had to admit that Donna had never disturbed him about anything but business when he was busy. Not that Donna was unfriendly, but she was very focused on her job and, now that he gave it some thought, on his job. Since both were early birds, over the coffee and danishes the two agreed to meet each morning before the start of the workday to review the upcoming day and requests from others the day before.

In the evening, before she left, Donna would also send Peter an e-mail message that summarized phone calls and visitors to his office he missed while he was busy during the day, so he would be ready the very next morning to attend to these issues.

Donna's experience suggests:

- **Drop the hints.** Better to tell your boss, "We have a problem here." People who are too busy to stop what they are doing to hear you out aren't likely to pick up on hints—and rude remarks only irritate further those who are already stressed out.

- **Keep your conversations short.** If you can, limit your requests or observations to ten seconds. When you practice the ten-second rule, you get your boss to focus directly on the issue at hand, and you make it clear that your objective in the communication is for your boss to take some action, and that you are not trying to take a piece of your boss's busy day away from her.

Given stressful workdays, here are some other rules that minimize the likelihood of conflicts:

- **Take notes.** Show your boss that you respect her time by writing down instructions or other information so you don't have to ask her to repeat her directions. If you have questions, ask them then and there.

- **Respect deadlines.** When you meet the deadlines imposed on you by your boss, you enable her to make her deadlines. However, this means that you accept only those deadlines that you know you can meet. One way that you can trigger conflicts between you and your boss is to agree to complete critical work on a specific date, knowing very well the date is unrealistic given your other workload. Better to be open with your boss; discuss your other assignments, and together come up with a plan that will enable you to complete the most critical work on time, even if it means bringing in a temp or part-timer to take some of your load off your shoulders.

Let's say that you had a deadline and a plan to meet it. But at the last minute your boss gives you a critical project that distracts you from the earlier deadline. Let's take this situation even further. Your boss blows up when he learns that you won't complete the earlier assignment on schedule. You have two choices here: You can give back in kind, trying to win the argument by outshouting your boss, or you can give your boss time to yell, then calmly explain that your initial plans were thrown off as you tried to do too many things at once, and develop then and there a plan to achieve both objectives or, at least, the project of greater priority.

One other point: In a situation like this, the best course of all would have been to have prevented the problem from ever happening. Even if you initially think you can complete both assignments on schedule, as soon as the impossibility of this becomes evident, you should bring the situation to your boss's attention. Either a decision could have been made about which task to give priority, or a plan could have been hatched by you both to complete both projects on schedule, perhaps by asking help from another assistant or bringing a temp into the office to handle your routine work while you focused on these projects.

Many work-related conflicts that occur between an office professional and her boss are triggered by surprises that either embarrass the boss or otherwise put him in a poor light. You can minimize the likelihood of such conflicts by seeing that your boss is informed of the status of projects, particularly any operational or political problems you are encountering in your work, mistakes you or another person have made (with an action plan to remedy it to ensure that you don't suffer the fate of messengers of bad news), or information that affects your boss professionally or even personally (even information about your boss that is on the office grapevine, without letting him know the source of your knowledge).

- **Be deferential.** The more volatile your workplace, the more sensitive people are. Your boss is no exception. He will expect to be treated with the respect that comes with his position, and doing so can improve your relationship with him. You can show your respect both by your words—"I would appreciate your feedback" or "Okay, boss, what do I do next?"—and by your deeds—supporting your boss in a team meeting rather than joining with other factions on an issue.

The Issue of Empowerment

Some managers have a clear understanding of what empowerment entails and are ready to empower their assistants; others aren't as clear about what it entails or as willing to empower their office professionals. Your manager may fall in one category or the other or somewhere in between. Likewise, you may want all the authority that your boss is willing to give or you may be content in a traditional secretarial or administrative assistant position, or somewhere in between. Differences can arise when you and your boss are at different points on the empowerment question. In particular, problems can arise if you are looking to be fully empowered, defining empowerment as "freedom to make decisions beyond my job description," whereas your boss's definition of empowerment goes no further than "freedom to make decisions and take actions without direction within her job limits," although problems can also arise where bosses are more than willing to empower their assistants yet unwilling or unable to do so because of budgetary constraints that prevent bosses from rewarding assistants for taking on the additional responsibilities.

Here are some tips to help you under either circumstances:

- **Be upfront about your demands.** Ask for what you want. I recently spoke before a group of administrative assistants on the subject of empowerment, and it did not come as a surprise to me that many of the group who wanted to be empowered had yet to bring up their desire with their boss or that those who were already empowered had not discussed opportunities for recognition, if not more money than more training opportunities.

- **Approach your dilemma from a problem-solving mindset.** Don't come into your boss's office ready for a fight. You will only get one. Rather, come in with your request to take on some specific assignment, some of the reasons why it makes sense for your manager to agree, and finally two or three ways in which you can both make it happen. You are less likely to get a defensive or, worse, confrontational response if you put your request in the context of why this would benefit your boss.

- **Build your case before making a demand.** Prepare your boss in advance for a request for a new job title or additional pay in recognition of the extra work you've assumed, rather than hit him cold with the demand. Don't say, "I want . . . ," but rather, "Over the last year, I've assumed more work, taking on supervision of a part-time assistant as well as purchasing office supplies, acting as liaison with systems and sometimes repairing the equipment myself, training staff on new software, and the like. I would like to be recognized for this additional work. So I would like . . . ." When you have given your boss reason to consider your request, you minimize the likelihood of a blowup.

Incidentally, the same advice applies if you are making a request to be empowered. Set aside time on your boss's calendar to discuss your request so you will have your boss's full attention. Even a reluctant boss should be willing to give your request a try, and should be unlikely to lose her temper, if you offer an action plan that has you taking on increasing responsibility in small steps.

Bad Bosses

Some bosses are just difficult to work with. Bill is a case in point.

The verbal abuser

I wish I could say that Andrea's boss was verbally abusive to her because he was under so much work stress. But truth is, Bill is an abusive boss in good times and bad, during periods of calm and periods of stress, using words in a way that another person might use their fists to feel superior over another. When a problem arose in the office, it was always Andrea's fault. He would tell her that she was "incompetent," that she was "unprofessional," and that she was "incapable of handling his work." In time, Andrea began to believe Bill. After awhile, her work began to be affected, in truth; she had begun to believe Bill that all the problems experienced in the department were, indeed, her own fault.

Truth came out when Andrea was assigned a second boss, besides Bill. Unlike Bill, who never acknowledged any of Andrea's accomplishments, Ted recognized the worth in Andrea's work and gave credit where it was due. Andrea had been working for both Bill and Ted for several months when she suddenly realized the impact of Bill's hurtful words on her self-esteem. Sorely tempted to give back to Bill his remarks in kind, instead Andrea took her problem to Ted, who advised her to take the situation to the human resources department.

Because he had been present on several occasions when Bill had verbally abused her, and could vouch for the quality of her performance, Ted agreed to go with her to support her case.

Since verbal abusers often don't know that they are guilty of the offense, confronting the situation in an assertive manner infrequently works. Often the only solution in a situation where the manager's behavior is chronic is for the office professional to bring the problem to the attention of human resources and, if they fail to dismiss the manager, for the assistant to move elsewhere within the organization or leave.

Other situations lend themselves better to the advice offered in Section I of this book about defusing conflicts; that is, calmly address the difference in opinion seeking a common ground for discussion and resolution of the problem. Let's look at some other difficult bosses and how this formula might work with them.

The poor communicator

This boss may know what she wants done, but she never makes it clear to those who report to her. If you are her assistant, you are frustrated by her failure to share information with you that you need to do your work well, let alone her inability to explain what she wants done. In

Chapter 5, we mentioned how some people—"conceptualizers"—often talk in abstract terms. This boss would seem to fall in this category based on her vague, infrequent, or unclear directions.

You might want to scream at your boss, "What the h--- do you want me to do?" but, instead, schedule a meeting with this boss at which you can tell her, "I'm concerned that I may not be meeting the goals you have for my work. Could we discuss how we could more clearly communicate with one another about the work you want done?" Listen to your boss's response to see if you can understand why she isn't clear and encourage better communications. Try to set up meetings with your boss at least once a week to review the steps she wants you to take. If your boss seems resistant to any such suggestion, don't press. Rather than make the situation worse, accept the fact that you must either learn to operate with less information than you feel you need, and perhaps have to redo work as a consequence, or search elsewhere for another boss who is clearer about work to be done.

The workaholic

This boss not only sets high expectations for himself but expects staff members to assume the same heavy workload, even though the added work is affecting your home life or health or both. Because this manager demands of himself as much as he demands of you, you may want to meet with your boss to determine if there are extraordinary pressures on him to achieve a goal, and whether the pressure on him and you will lessen once the objective is met. If you find that this is just your boss's style, then you need to identify solutions to the added work and present those to your boss for consideration. Complaining will get you nowhere; an action plan, even if it calls for extra help, can get the work done and the pressure off your shoulders.

The scaredy cat

This boss won't go off on a limb for you, whether it's for a well-deserved raise or new job title, or even a training program that will make you more efficient over the longer term. This boss assumes that his superior "will never go for it," and won't even try, which means that other departments have the latest technology, more staff than your department, or other resources that ensure that work gets done efficiently and effectively. The scaredy cat procrastinates until the very last minute and then makes decisions based on whose argument is most forceful.

To get what you want or your department needs from the scaredy cat, don't confront him; like any cornered feline, he may claw you, then purr an apology. It is better to allay his fears about making a request when they arise by assuring the scaredy cat that there is no need to worry—"Senior management will appreciate your bringing our need to its attention"—by helping to build the scaredy cat's self-confidence by pointing up the benefits of some action he plans to take—"All your staff agree that we need to upgrade to the new software package systems"—and by repeatedly pointing to the merits of some stand your scaredy cat is thinking of taking—"Your boss will be impressed with your initiative on this project."

The loafer

Your boss gets the recognition, but all you have to do is to compare her office, which is spotless, and her desk, which is clean, to your work station, which is crowded with files and reports yet done, and your desk, which is stacked high with projects to complete, to get an appreciation of who is more productive. Accusing the loafer of dumping work on you will only lead to an argument about who's the boss. Rather than accuse your boss of not pulling her weight, or challenge your manager's right to give you work, raise questions about where your authority ends and your boss's begins: "I may do work that misdirects the project and the project may fail as a consequence. Let's be clear about your tasks and mine." Rather than stomp off angered by the added workload, keep in mind that the more responsibility you get from the loafer, the more opportunity you have to show the rest of your organization your full capabilities.

Use working for a loafer to empower yourself.

8

Dealing with Co-Workers

It's as important to be on good terms with your co-workers as it is to have a good working relationship with your own supervisor and other managers in your organization. Positive collegial relationships include not only your counterparts in other departments but staff members within and outside your department and support personnel like systems experts, mail clerks, the telephone operators, and the janitorial staff.

Sowing the Seeds of Positive Work Relationships

Ideally, everyone in your organization is pulling in the same direction, collaborating and cooperating to achieve the company's business plan and strategic goals. But in the real world, problems arise from mixed messages, personality differences, and real and not-so-real (think political or turf) dilemmas. Your first goal should be to prevent conflicts with co-workers. Should differences arise, your second objective should be to resolve the problem before it escalates and impairs your ability to do your work, unnecessarily distracts you from your job, and even creates factions for and against you that make the workplace stressful not only for you but everyone around you—including your boss. You want the same kind of partnership with colleagues as you have with your boss, one based on mutual respect and cooperation.

Admittedly, such a relationship with each and every one of your co-workers won't come easily. Built on trust and respect, it does not occur instantaneously. It can develop, however, as you demonstrate to others in your organization that they can rely on your support. Although there is no guarantee that practice of the Golden Rule in your dealings with others—"Do unto others as you would expect them to do unto you"—will be returned in kind. But the alternative on your part—"Do to others what others have done to you"—will guarantee fuss and fury between you and those you've "done to," because this means that co-workers are treating each other unprofessionally or disrespectfully.

Collegial Problems

The kinds of problems that occur among employees fall into four general categories: communications, turf and territory, professionalism, and interpersonal issues. Let's look at these in greater depth.

Communications

In Chapter 4, the impact of both verbal and nonverbal communications on creation and resolution of conflicts was described. It's not only what we say but how we say it that determines whether our relationships with others are positive or negative. Beyond verbal and body language, conflicts may occur between you and another when messages are distorted by jammed communication channels or a third person in your company who distorts your comments either consciously or unconsciously. For instance, you may need some information from systems but fail to get it because your name was never added to the distribution list for such communications. Or you may have told Mollie that you have been late in making deadlines lately because of your heavy workload, but all Mollie heard you say was that you are always late in making deadlines and that's what she's telling everyone you said. Or you might have told a co-worker that you wanted to apply for a promotion but didn't plan to do so because human resources might have to tell your boss, and now, your simple concern has grown on the grapevine: the grapevine says you don't trust human resources not to tell your boss and that, consequently, you chose not to apply for a promotion. Further, the human resources manager has heard the rumor, and now all you can get from him is monosyllabic responses to your requests.

Turf and territoriality

As organizations reorganize, then reorganize again, ambiguities can arise about who does what. In situations in which people don't know if they will have a job the next week, individuals can become defensive about their authority and possessive of their responsibilities. In your dealings with your boss, as we mentioned in Chapter 7, conflicts may arise as you are asked to assume more responsibility without some corresponding recognition in the form of a title or raise. Likewise, in your dealings with co-workers, problems can arise as you take on work that previously was not considered yours. Other office professionals may resent your advancement. Staff members may refuse to do as you ask, treating you as "just a secretary," because either they aren't cognizant of your new responsibilities (due to lack of communication from your boss) or they refuse to accept the realities of the new workplace where office professionals are assuming greater roles. On Secretary's Day, Lenore found herself the butt of jokes from two staff members. When she came to her desk, she found Gene in her seat, fiddling with the roses her boss had given her. In a falsetto voice, he said, "Oh, I'm so happy; this is my day." "Honey," said George, seated on her desk, "you've never looked prettier."

Both Gene and George had been told to *assist* Lenore in updating the department procedures and policies manual, and, she told me, they didn't take well to having to accept directions from her. In the past, it had been their job, and they saw her leadership of the team as an intrusion onto their turf.

Professionalism

Looking at the Lenore situation from her perspective, George's and Gene's behavior was an insult to her image of herself as an office professional. She was sorely tempted to reciprocate by neglecting to provide the clerical support the two office clowns expected from her.

Lenore is very sensitive about her own position yet she violates others' sense of professionalism, treating members of the mailroom staff and janitorial service with little respect. She continually mislays her office telephone directory and consequently is always calling the switchboard for help, but in her rush to get her work done she has yet to say "thank you" to the operators for their help.

She's "more sinned against than a sinner" when it comes to systems support in the form of Rick. He's the most knowledgeable person in systems about the company's more sophisticated word processing programs, but he is also the least sought for help because he treats anyone whose computer he services, whether manager or employee, as a computer illiterate. Rick knows that Lenore has several new programs she wants to master, yet he is constantly teasing her about mistakes she makes rather than offering to help her increase her computer skills.

Lenore's department is clearly a garden in which conflicts could grow.

Interpersonal relationships

Differences—from ethnic, religious, and gender issues to family relationships and favorite hobbies—can trigger conflicts. It's hard to believe, but Phyllis, the administrative assistant to the president and a grandmother, is forever making negative comparisons between herself and her unmarried co-workers who "lack the love and support of a happy family to go home to." At another company, Roy, an administrative professional, has little to talk about during lunch with his female co-workers; he's interested in sports—baseball, football, basketball, you name it—but his female colleagues get enough talk about sports at home from their husbands. Roy sulks. Caught up in their discussions about the latest movies they've seen, the women are oblivious to him. This is unfortunate for everyone because Roy has other interests in common with his co-workers that he could share—he loves mysteries like Martha, has a two-year-old son like Darlene's brother, has done community theater like Blair, and is considering graduate school like Elsie.

These are the kinds of situations that can trigger conflicts if nothing is done about them. What can you do?

Resolving Collegial Conflicts

Different problems demand different solutions. Let's look at some remedies and the kinds of problems they are most suited to address:

- **Never order people about.** This is advice for Lenore. Issuing brusque commands will alienate your co-workers, making it unlikely that they will lend you a hand when you most need it. Especially if you lack the positional power to demand someone do a task for you, a polite request is more likely to achieve your goal than a barked demand.

- **Establish a common ground.** This bit of advice might seem manipulative, but colleagues are more likely to work with you rather than against you if you flatter them. And one of the most effective forms of flattery is to quote your colleague in a complimentary manner. If Lenore wants help from Rick, she might want to say something like, "You know, Rick, this reminds me of the time you said we needed to find a new platform for our network . . . ." Or, talking to George and Gene, Lenore might suggest to them, "You guys are most familiar with the procedural manual. Given your experience, you can help me by recommending an action plan for my consideration."

- **Don't tell tales.** You don't want to contribute to the office grapevine. So be tactful in conversations with your peers. Don't say anything you would not want to have repeated by another. Also, while it may be tempting to be in the know about grapevine chatter, your participation, even merely as a listener and spreader of news, can build ill will and a reputation for untrustworthiness.

- **Learn to admit your own shortcomings and mistakes and ask for help.** Rick, for instance, is knowledgeable about the company's systems. All right, he likes to tease Lenore about the mistakes she makes. But she can raise their conversation to a professional level by saying, "Rick, I seem to keep making a mistake here, and I wonder if you've got any insights on how I can avoid this problem." In putting Rick into a superior position, Lenore ends up the winner—she gains an ally who has reason to help her. And she has given Rick an opportunity to prove he is as knowledgeable about the company's computer programs as he thinks he is.

- **Mirror the other person's movements.** If you and a colleague are having words, you can defuse the conflict by subtly copying the other person's gestures, even her breathing. Just as rephrasing and restating another's words can establish a common ground, so, too, can mirroring their gestures.

- **Don't put on airs.** Yes, it may be true that your responsibilities have grown, but playing one-upmanship with peers will only foster resentment and encourage your colleagues to withhold key information or help. Find something interesting about what the other person is doing and talk about that, downplaying your own work when it seems appropriate to do so.

- **Make small talk work for you.** Roy, Martha, Darlene, Blair, and Elsie have many things in common, but they won't discover them until one or more of them are willing to discover what they have in common with each other. Gaining the support of colleagues on potentially challenging initiatives can be difficult. If you push too hard, you can irritate co-workers. Better to build connections with co-workers based on personal interests, not just professional needs, so you can make an emotional appeal for their support.

- **Use humor when appropriate.** When Lenore approached her desk and found Gene in her seat and George seated on her desk, she might have wanted to resolve her conflict with them by punching them out. But a better approach might be to join in the fun. Humor can be a powerful weapon for building allies, particularly when it is used to show others that you don't take yourself too seriously and aren't out to make their lives more difficult than they are. In Lenore's case, she could have told Gene that he could share the roses, since he seemed to like them so much, if he agreed to answer her phone during her lunch, or she could have told George what a great paperweight he made for her desk. A shared laugh is comparable to a favorite song, movie, or book, in building rapport between people.

- **Don't ask directly for support if there seems to be a chance that doing so will trigger a conflict.** Watch the other person's body language. If he is fidgeting or looking away from you or otherwise showing signs of discomfort or anger, then back off and elicit suggestions for your plan rather than ask directly for help. Let's say that you have a major mailing to get out and you need a hand from another office professional. As you approach her, you see she is looking away from you and has a grimace on her face. She's on her way to lunch and is eager to leave. If you ask for her help right now, she's going to say no. Instead, go to her and ask if she has any thoughts on how you can get started by gathering the stationery supplies you'll need and having the handbill printed. Thank her for her ideas. At least, neither of you will have cause to feel angry with one another. At best, your co-worker may offer to lend the needed hand when she returns from lunch.

- **Avoid hostility by reframing the conversation.** Your colleague is short-tempered and ready for a fight. You aren't aware of it when you come up to him with your question. He needs a target, and it seems as if it will be you. Your day hasn't been much better than your co-worker's. You can let this individual's hostility trigger your own anger, or you can paraphrase his remarks to prove you were listening to his complaint, add a sympathetic comment that does not take sides, and conclude by stating your initial query in a manner that suggests a common concern.

- **End feuding before it even begins.** You don't want to play a Hatfield to a co-worker's McCoy. You have too much work to get done to waste your energy in a workplace feud that could be potentially damaging to your career. (Managers may occasionally have to mediate between staff members but they don't like to play the role, and they especially don't like to play the role if the other party in the conflict is from another department.) Rather than let a co-worker stay ticked off with you, apologize and get back to work. Even if you weren't at fault, your willingness to let bygones be bygones outclasses your co-worker.

- **Keep in mind that you can never undo what you said.** It's better not to say something that will alienate another employee. Avoid beginning long-term grudges or short-term miscommunications by holding your own counsel. Take a deep breath before giving a colleague a piece of your mind. Find a means of resolving the disagreement other than unloading on your peer, no matter the temptation to tell her what you think of her. For instance, Mollie has made others question your professionalism, but you have to ask yourself if it was a misunderstanding or a deliberate effort to sabotage your career. In either case, what can losing your cool in public with Mollie get you but a further bad rep?

- **Confront issues privately.** If you must confront Mollie over her comments, then do so where you won't be playing in front of an audience. A discussion of someone's shortcomings—whether yours or Mollie's—has no place in the hallways or in front of other colleagues or customers.

- **Be clear about your relationship with others.** Let's say you tell another office professional, "Would you please collate these sheets together, then place them in these addressed envelopes?" Your colleague responds, "No, I have my own work to get done," then she gets on with her job. This is a conflict but it isn't about getting a mailing done; rather, it's about whether you have the authority to *tell* a co-worker to do a job. If you can tell your co-worker to complete the mailing, you can also tell her to do other departmental work. Her response is to the implication that you have authority over her. Until you both agree on the nature of your relationship—what is a fair request, what is an imposition, and what can be demanded—you and your colleague will continue to clash.

- **Know where boundaries start and end.** You may be above issues of turf, seeing territorial battles in your organization as petty, willing to let others operate in your turf without permission, but others may not be so open-minded. If your intrusion into another's territory is likely to trigger a conflict, respect their boundaries and get off their turf immediately. If you need to go outside your own area to accomplish an objective, and "outside" represents another person's area of responsibility, speak to her first. Either ask the person to cooperate by doing the work herself for you or get her permission to do the work yourself even though it falls within her territory.

Here's a case in point. Irene had been asked by her boss to put together a meeting of his colleagues from the sales department and two members of a client firm. Stan is in accounting, but in a casual conversation with the client firm's CEO he had come up with an idea that could have meant more business for the client firm and his own company. The CEO suggested that Stan put together a meeting between his company's senior sales personnel and his own vice-presidents of marketing and sales within the next two weeks, by which time the client's firm would have to submit its budget for the year to headquarters. Enthusiastic about his idea, Stan had told Irene to get the calendars for the firm's top salespeople through their assistant Maryanne.

Irene knew that Stan was pleased about the reception to his idea. The firm had had some bad fiscal months, and there was the threat of a downsizing hanging over staff. This added business could mean the difference. So she quickly e-mailed Maryanne with the request and a brief explanation of the reason for her request.

Instead of the information she needed for Stan, she received three e-mail responses: one from Maryanne and one each from the two sales executives. Each message pointed to the strategic relationship between her firm and client company and the importance of future discussions under direction of the sales department. Despite his best intentions, Stan had intruded on others' turf. Although Irene was only following Stan's instructions, the tone in Maryanne's e-mail message tempted her to counterattack.

- **Clarify, don't counterattack.** Fortunately, both Stan and Irene appreciated the pressures on their colleagues. Stan sent an e-mail message to both his colleagues explaining his casual meeting and the subsequent discussion. He had been asked to put together a meeting, he said, but had no objection about putting the project back into the hands of the sales department. Irene did likewise with her co-worker. She e-mailed Maryanne, explained why Stan felt it was important to get the group together within the next two weeks, and apologized if it seemed as if she were stepping on Maryanne's operating area.

This advice is applicable to one-on-one conversations, regardless of their nature. If someone insults you, counterattacking only ratchets up the argument to the next level. Rather, ignore the insult, regardless of its intent, and pursue the conversation. Not letting the retort trigger a remark in kind ends the argument before it can even start; if there are onlookers, it leaves the other person embarrassed.

- **Ignore insults.** Sometimes ignoring the insult isn't sufficient. The other party is determined to argue with you, and he continues to bait you. Rick in systems has been known to do this with office professionals, continually putting them down to get them to lose their temper. Lenore has come up with a list of responses to Rick's barbs that have proven effective. Since she is hot tempered herself, Lenore has printed them and tacked them to her cubicle wall: "That's your opinion." "You're entitled to your view." "That may be your perception." "I don't really have time right now to get into the problem with you." and "You must be having a really bad day today."

If these don't work, Lenore knows that leveling with Rick about how his remarks make her feel will end them. In a similar situation, be as direct as you can: "It sounds as if you think I am incompetent?" "Did you intend to insult me?" "Are you aware how you are making me feel?" Often questions like these not only will put an end to the insults but prompt an airing of the true problem between you and the other person.

- **Get to the heart of the conflict.** Once you and the other person are prepared to discuss the conflict openly, stop asking further questions and let the other party know how her conduct has made you feel: "I would have appreciated your letting me know when you planned to come to fix my computer." "I need your support until I've mastered these newer software programs." Only ask questions if you really need more information: "What book would you suggest on these software programs I purchased?" "Do you know about any training program I might attend?"

Some Specific Problems

Let's look at some specific problem-peers and how you should respond to their behavior before the situation gets out of hand:

- **The rumor monger.** He gossips about everyone in the organization, filling gaps of information with his imagination. Much of what he adds to the rumor mill is inaccurate, which includes stories about you. If you confront the rumor monger, he's likely to become defensive and deny having said anything. Consequently, before you talk to the rumor monger, verify the facts: what was said, how was it said, to whom was it said, and when was it said. Make it difficult for this gossiper to deny his role. If you said one thing to someone and your comments are being misrepresented, you may want to bring the person who told you about the rumor to the individual to whom you originally made the comment, and clarify the confusion. Nip the likelihood of a conflict with others in the bud.

- **The assistant who doesn't assist.** You are willing to lend others a hand, and most of your colleagues are willing to do the same for you except one assistant who doesn't carry a fair share of the load, gets away with as little as possible, promises to help or cooperate but never keeps those promises, and otherwise isn't a team player. Your association with this person has proved that you can't count on this individual, but today you have a major project to complete and you have asked the person to cover for you. The person agrees and then doesn't keep her promise.

You want to tell your friends and, together with them, tell this person off, but realize that not all the other assistants will support you, and you may split the assistants into factions on your side and hers. The support the person gets will also make her feel her inaction was further justified—"after all, you volunteered for all that extra work." Instead, talk to the person and discuss the consequences of her behavior to you, to her other co-workers, and to herself. Stay calm as you cite the circumstances: "The board of directors was meeting and my boss was asked by the CEO if I could complete the typing and reproduction of a critical report by this afternoon. I asked you to help me by finishing the report that my boss needed for tomorrow's senior staff meeting and you promised to do it this afternoon. You never did the work, which means I will have to stay late tonight to do the report. This is just one example of your lack of cooperation. We all need to pull together if we're to get the work done."

If your co-worker makes an effort to help you, reinforce that positive behavior by acknowledging it. If she seems deaf to your feelings, don't ask for help in the future—you know what you can expect. Don't ignore her; treat her as you treat your other co-workers. But don't set up circumstances that will give you cause to lose your temper with her and divide the staff on the issue.

- **The empire builder.** Unlike the deadweight previously mentioned, the empire builder welcomes increased responsibility, but her goal is to increase her personal power base, not increase department productivity. To achieve her purpose, she will stab you and other peers in the back, denigrating your abilities to those who make the high-visibility assignments. Before your relationship with the empire builder reaches conflict stage, confront her. Be specific, clear, and demonstrate your unwillingness to be a pawn in her effort to advance herself. Don't allow her to muddy your reputation and thereby take opportunities from you for advancement. Clarify any misunderstandings with your boss as soon as you learn about their existence; don't complain about your empire-building peer. Rather, put the problem in management terms: Empire building erodes collaboration and cooperation within an organization and creates an environment in which conflicts can arise that can lower productivity.

9

Good Customer Relationships

Stories about rudeness, indifference, or discourteousness to a customer spread quickly. Customers who feel they were poorly treated by someone within an organization will tell, on average, about 20 people—relatives, friends, and neighbors—about their experience. Each of these individuals, in turn, may tell at least half that number what the unhappy or dissatisfied customer told them.

That means the tale of just one unpleasant contact between a member of an organization and one of its customers can be heard by at least 201 individuals, subsequently influencing everyone's feelings about the company and the people in it.

We all know that this bad word of mouth can influence both the acquisition of new customers and retention of existing ones. But it has another effect as well: It can affect the expectations and behaviors of these individuals when they meet with or talk over the phone to members of the organization. When we hear good news about a company, as customers we are more apt to speak courteously to their representatives, even if we are bringing complaints to their attention. On the other hand, if a friend, relative, or a neighbor tells us that he was treated unpleasantly by a company, and had to yell or scream to get service, then we are more likely to yell and scream, too, on the assumption that that is the only way to get action from the firm.

Consequently, it's important that we deal with customers in a courteous manner. Even if a customer is upset, we need to maintain our composure and handle the situation in a professional manner. We shouldn't allow their agitation to trigger our own anger and thereby permit a conflict to develop. After all, it only makes our jobs or the jobs of others in our organization more difficult.

Admittedly, it's easy to deal with satisfied customers. It's not so easy to handle those with excessive demands or complaints, but handling the situation well can turn a dissatisfied customer into a satisfied—and continued—customer.

A study by the U.S. Office of Consumer Affairs found that 72 percent of customers come back if their complaints are resolved quickly. On the other hand, 81 percent won't come back if they complain but their complaint isn't resolved. The key issue isn't that the complaint is resolved or not resolved, however, but that it is resolved *quickly*—46 percent of customers don't come back even if their complaint is resolved, because they had to come back again and again for satisfaction, ultimately kicking and screaming, to get resolution of their problem.

Besides, hearing out a customer with a complaint can be a learning opportunity for your firm. It may take lots of patience on your part to listen to an upset customer (many customers need time to get past venting to get to the specific point of their dissatisfaction), but listening may identify some specific fault in your firm's product or service, or policies that needs to be changed. Over the long run this can have tremendous benefit if the knowledge is shared with those who need to know—your boss or the head of sales, customer service, product development, or engineering, to name a few key areas.

Because this book is about conflicts, this chapter will focus on how best to handle angry customers, but the advice is helpful in any customer contact. It's based on a single idea: Make each and every customer or client with whom you interact feel special. Just as learning from another about bad treatment by a firm can influence a client's behavior, so can your initial contact with a client shape the customer's attitude and behavior in a positive way. An upbeat, affirming, personable, and respectful attitude almost obligates the client to reciprocate.

The Cause for Upset

When a client visits or calls to discuss a problem, the complaint may have to do with a flaw in the product or quality of service offered. But the emotional temperature of the client may have less to do with product than with other factors—some tied to personal problems, some to past interactions with your business, some to your professional demeanor or manner in discussing the problem with the customer. As I mentioned, a considerate attitude can prompt consideration in kind; however, it works the other way as well—defensiveness or anger or some other unpleasant behavior can trigger a similar response by a customer. In Monica's case, it wasn't that she was distant with Helga, the assistant to the CEO of one of the firm's biggest clients. Monica tried everything she could to thaw the assistant.

Yes, product had shipped several days later than Monica's company had told Helga's company it would, but Monica had been able to pull strings with the shipping company, and the order would arrive only one day later than promised, but still two days before Helga admitted they would need the product. Monica understood that Helga's boss and Helga had cause to be upset—their expectations weren't being met—but she felt she had done all she could. Still, it wasn't appreciated. It wasn't until they met at a meeting of office professionals months later that Monica discovered that Helga had been going through a difficult period then—her mother had been placed in a nursing home, her marriage was breaking up, and her boss was talking about retiring, which could have threatened her job.

Here are other reasons that can predispose a customer to be upset before you even pick up the phone or begin a conversation face to face with them:

- The customer has already been transferred several times on the phone by your colleagues and has no intention of being treated disrespectfully by another member of your organization.
- The customer has always felt insecure or victimized, or otherwise powerless, and believes that the only way he can get his way is to make a ruckus as soon as you pick up the phone.

- The customer thinks yelling and screaming and otherwise making noise will get her what she wants, whether it is a replacement for the current product or treatment contrary to your company's policy.

- The customer believes that you aren't knowledgeable enough either about his problem, your corporate policies, or your organization to handle the situation correctly. He expects not to get his problem resolved correctly and he's already prepared to fight over the matter.

- The customer feels that you aren't listening to her even if you are.

- You may have been distracted with some other problem when you picked up the phone or greeted the customer, and she may feel that your initial response is indicative of your interest in her situation. She's not willing to let you make amends for your brief distraction.

- You may have raised a question, and it may have been according to policy, but the customer may think that you are doubting his integrity or honesty. For instance, your company may require that customers be questioned about broken products to determine engineering flaws, but the query may make the customer think that you think he broke it when using it incorrectly.

- The customer may be responding to the tone of your voice, and that tone may be a reflection of something happening in your life (like a problem with your boss or spouse or children).

- Like Helga, the customer has been promised something and that promise hasn't been kept. The customer expects you to make other promises that could be as empty or as unkept as the earlier one.

The advice offered to help you calm the customer and resolve the problem—and avoid a conflict—is based on five needs of all customers:

1. Customers want to be treated with respect. If they have a problem, they want you to show a caring attitude.

2. Customers want to be taken seriously. Their problem isn't a joke—not to them—and they don't want to feel that it is a joke to you.

3. Customers want their problems resolved so they never recur. Sometimes that entails simply assuring the customer that you will report the situation to the proper person. Regardless, the customer wants some sense that action will be taken on their need or dilemma.

4. Customers want immediate action. It may be five in the after-noon but they want some sign that you will address their demand immediately.

5. Customers want proof that they are being listened to. When they doubt they are being heard, they will create a ruckus if they think that is the only way to get your attention.

"So What Should I Do?"

When you meet with a customer, you want to present a positive personal appearance. You also should recognize that your body language could be countering what you are saying.

To convince a dissatisfied customer that you are able to solve a problem, you need to come across as a professional. That will be measured not only by your words but your appearance—your grooming and wardrobe—and your posture, movement, and gestures.

Even on dress-down days, your hair should be clean, brushed or combed, and well kept. Your clothing should be neat and clean. Your hands and fingernails should be clean. If you know that you will be meeting with customers on a specific day, even if it is dress-down, consider wearing less informal clothes than you might otherwise wear for the day. Keep in mind that those with whom you interact will be making decisions about you within five to ten seconds of meeting you. If your appearance isn't appropriate to your position and business, a customer is likely to worry about your ability to handle his demand and may ask to speak to a higher authority.

No matter how much reassurance you may offer that you are knowl-edgeable about the product and corporate policies, and that you can handle the individual's need, all you are likely to do is make a satisfied customer a little unsure about the service he's getting and an upset customer further agitated about his problem.

If you think presentation doesn't count, put yourself in a customer's shoes for a second. Let's assume that you received a mistake on your utility bill and you decide to go to the utility to remedy the mistake.

There are two clerks who can handle your problem. One woman is dressed in tight-fitting jeans and a t-shirt and sneakers. Her hair is swept up but strands are falling in her face as she sits at the desk biting her nails. There are stacks of paper scattered all around her desk.

What about the other clerk? She's dressed in a neatly pressed blouse and skirt. She's wearing flats and her nails are polished. Her desk has an equal amount of documents on it but the paperwork is organized in several neat stacks. Which of these two clerks would you prefer to handle your problem?

Let's take this situation one step further. Assume that the more disorganized individual offers to help you. Imagine your reaction.

Likely you would worry about how qualified this person is to handle your case. You might become defensive even before the person reaches for your bill. You may allow the clerk who has offered to help to assist you but you may raise your voice and a ruckus in order to get the attention of the other clerk, because you think that she could probably help your clerk handle your problem more expeditiously. In actuality, that other neatly dressed clerk may be brand-new and may know nothing about how to handle your account, but you won't know that. Your assessment is based on the appearance of the two clerks.

Body Language

What if the clerk who will handle your problem has a scowl on her face as she approaches you or, worse, looks away as you describe your need as if she doesn't consider your demand worth her attention? Any customer would be turned off by this response to their desire for service, but dissatisfied customers expect those to whom they bring their complaint to have a calm, concerned, interested facial expression, and not to appear as if they are distracted or consider the problem you bring to their attention indicative of your lack of intelligence.

When you meet with an unhappy customer, your facial expression should tell the customer that you care about his dilemma. You don't want the first impression that a customer gets is that you couldn't care one iota about him.

To send the message to any customer that you want to help, you should stand or sit straight as you speak with her. You don't loll or slouch, either of which could give the impression of disinterest or inattentiveness. When dealing with a dissatisfied customer, don't cross your arms in front of your chest or, if you are seated, cross your legs. These body gestures suggest a closed attitude and an unwillingness to listen. Rather, open your arms and lean toward the customer to show you are listening and have an open mind to her demands.

Don't crowd an upset customer, however. It can escalate her anger. Touching an upset person, particularly if she seems ready to lose control, can only set her off. It could even lead to a violent action on an angry customer's part.

If you need to get some records or other documents to help a customer, go directly for them. Don't stop to chat with a co-worker unless it has to do with the customer. This advice applies regardless of the customer situation. Such cavalier behavior can cause an upset and irritated customer to go ballistic, but it also can turn a contented customer into an unhappy one on the verge of going ballistic if the private conversation takes more than a few seconds' time.

I recently purchased some books. I had to stand in line for five to ten minutes before I reached the sales desk. There were several lines of customers and only a few clerks. When I came to the desk, the clerk took my books and my credit card, entered my computer number into the point-of-sales machine, and then turned to his off-duty friend and began a lengthy conversation. I stood there for a few minutes then spoke up, "I'm certain your friend has an interesting story but could you hear it after you have taken care of my purchase?" He answered, "The computer has to process your number."

It may have been true that his system was sluggish, and he was indeed waiting for the voucher, but that fact was immaterial. The sales clerk's behavior was sending a message to me that he didn't value my business enough to give me his attention. As I walked away, I was annoyed by the quality of the service and my own inability to come up with a clever retort to his response. I still buy books at the same store, but I must admit that I have stored up numerous "gotchas" in the event the situation recurs.

Calming a Customer on the Phone

Your appearance and body language won't matter if you are dealing with a distraught client on the phone. Since your client can't see the concern or interest on your face, you have to convey it with the tonal quality of your voice and the words you choose. If you have to look into some matter and then get back to the customer, it's imperative that you keep your promise. Otherwise, all you do is further upset the customer who may choose to go over your head, now with two complaints.

Sylvia, an office professional, felt that it was all right not to call by the time promised if she did not yet have the information that the customer requested. Not so. Even if the call had been simply to say that Sylvia had yet to get the information, it would have helped the nervous customer. No question, it's hard to keep track of such small promises, so you may want to get a small notebook where you list all promises to call back. You can note the time by which you promised to get back to the individual and the person's number along with the reason to call back.

Keep the notebook on your desk and visible to ensure you keep your promises. As you do so, you may want to check or cross out those promises made and kept.

The Wrong Tone

Attitude is communicated through voice tone. The tone of your voice should convey the message, "I'm here to help." This is especially important when dealing with angry or irritated customers. When your voice is annoyed, impatient, or condescending (like that sales clerk), then a customer will become annoyed. An already agitated customer will become more upset. Whether you are talking to a customer in person or on the phone, your voice should sound focused on her need and confident in your ability to resolve the dilemma. A tone of competence can calm an upset customer.

To improve the tonal quality of your voice, tape yourself in a conversation over the phone. In listening to the tape, check to see if your voice has the habit of going up at the end of a sentence, as if you are asking a question. That can communicate doubt in your ability. Practice so that your voice ends on a lower note.

Good Listening Habits

You should not interrupt a customer. Hear the person out. Upset customers won't be ready to discuss calmly their problem until they have had an opportunity to vent. Give them that chance. But don't tune them out in the interim. Listening to customers entails:

- Listening to facts *and* to feelings. Be aware of the emotional content as well as information.
- Focusing on the customer's comments, not the customer's communication style. So what if the customer has a stutter or a thick accent—don't let that distract you from the message.
- Not interrupting. In an already upset customer, this can induce more angry feelings.
- Looking the person in the face. You want the person to see that you are listening, which means giving the customer your full attention. Don't show your customer that you are interested in other things occurring in your vicinity by looking elsewhere. Look at the customer as she speaks.
- Keeping your own defensiveness out of the communication. If the customer is upset, he may use four-letter words, call you names, curse, or otherwise say unpleasant things. Don't let your emotional response to the customer's language or comments prevent you from helping the customer find a solution to his problem.
- Paraphrasing. Demonstrate that you have heard the customer by repeating in your own words what you have heard. Say, "Let me see if I understand your need (or problem) . . . ." Never tell an angry customer, "What you're trying to tell me is . . . ." Such phrasing might make the customer feel inarticulate.
- Taking notes. You don't want to write down everything that the customer says, but you might want to note further questions you wish to ask the customer. If the customer is speaking rapidly, and you aren't clear about some comment she has made, you may want to politely ask the customer to slow down.

"What Did You Say?"

You can trigger a conflict with a customer by what you say, as well as presentation, body language, tonal quality, and poor listening skills.

Let's say that a person is calling your firm to complain that she had sent in an order, given her credit card number, and was promised delivery in a week. Three weeks have passed, and the individual has yet to receive her order. You could say, "Do you have a problem with your card?" or you could say, "We have no record of your order being processed. Could you check to see if the credit card company processed payment for the order?"

Flip or sarcastic remarks only trigger a response in kind. You meant to commiserate or otherwise connect with the customer but all you have done, instead, is add to the tension.

Jokes are dangerous, too. You may think you are being funny but your small joke may fall flat and, instead, cause you to come across as rude or discourteous.

You may notice by the customer's manner that the specific problem goes beyond a late delivery or faulty gizmo, and you may want to make her feel better by offering some words of compassion or hope. Know that your words can come across as intrusive or as critical of the customer for taking her personal problem out on you. The customer feels she has the right to be upset or angry if she wants to be; being told otherwise will only make her more upset or angry.

Even a poorly worded statement can offend a customer, particularly one already upset. For instance, I hate to fill out forms, and I may make mistakes, but I don't want someone to remind me of it. Consequently, I would much prefer someone to tell me that there are a few areas on a form I still need to complete than be told by someone, "You did all this wrong." At the least, it could embarrass me; at worst, it could trigger defensiveness.

You certainly don't want to come across as fingerpointing with the finger in the customer's face. Use "I" rather than "you" in explaining what went awry. For instance, a client firm's director calls to tell you that some order was misdirected, and you check the records and see that the problem was due to the information provided by the client firm. You shouldn't say, "You made a mistake." Better to tell the director, "I can see that there is a confusion here." Or, "I see that there has been a mis-communication."

If you then are required, for example, to get a new form prepared to reship the order to the correct address, inform the director of the requirement as a request; never order a customer to do something. Say, "If you would please prepare another form and fax it, we can redirect the shipment"; don't tell him, "Fax me another copy of the corrected form and we'll take care of your problem."

If you want to prevent a recurrence of the situation, you may want to give the director instructions for filling out critical parts of the form. Phrase your instructions to focus on how the situation can be kept from recurring; you can only irritate a customer by reminding him that he did something wrong. Say, "When you fill out the form, check that the address is correct, include the telephone number of the facility," and so on. Don't say, "You should have proofed the form better. You should also have added a telephone number just in case you made a mistake with the address."

"Should" is a particularly dangerous word, likely to trigger a heated re-sponse in those already agitated. Other dangerous words are "always," "never," and "but." Ask yourself, for instance, how you might feel if one of your vendors told you that "your firm always pays late" or "your firm never thinks ahead about its supply needs." Or "I know you need a new keyboard tomorrow but . . . ."

When a customer calls, no matter your rapport with the individual, you shouldn't ask, "So what's your problem?" Even if your customer or client does, indeed, have a problem, she doesn't want to seem always incompetent, which your reply to her call suggests. Rather, say, "What can I do for you?"

When the customer tells you, practice some of the listening skills listed earlier. Paraphrase what you have heard. Be sure that you understand the customer's concern before you try to solve the problem. If you seem to be trying to solve the wrong problem, the customer will only become more upset. Ask the customer to slow down if you can't keep up with what she's saying. Ask the customer, "Let me see if I've got this straight . . . ."

Sometimes it's not you but rather the customer who isn't listening. You've told her that her request is impossible or unreasonable but she keeps asking for the same thing, just in different words. Let's go back to the situation between Monica and Helga. What if Monica offered to get the shipment to Helga's office by Thursday but Helga repeatedly said, "You promised it to us by Wednesday. We want it Wednesday"? All Monica could do would be to reframe her response each time to Helga's demand, explaining why her demand was impossible to satisfy. If Helga still did not appreciate the impossibility of her request, then Monica might have asked either to speak to Helga's boss or to ask Helga if she could call back after she had looked into the matter further, promising nothing.

That time away from the phone would give Monica an opportunity to double-check with her boss in case there was some way to satisfy Helga's demand. But, more important, it would also provide her with a cooling-off period.

When dealing with someone who is upset and maybe yelling and screaming, it's very easy to get caught up in the emotions and begin to lose your own temper. Just as in a tense team situation in which you might want to call time-out so that the group calms down, you may want to call time-out in a conflict with a customer to give yourself a chance to regain your composure. Excuse yourself politely. You could say, "Excuse me a moment while I check our corporate policy on this" or "I need to discuss how we can best handle this situation. I'll be just a moment . . . ."

Never use as an excuse to the customer that you have to handle another problem, merely to get some cooling-off time for yourself. Even if you do, indeed, have another crisis on your hands that demands your immediate attention, excuse yourself in a way that communicates your concern in the customer's situation.

The Problem Grows

Despite all you have said and offered to do to help the customer, the customer may still be dissatisfied. What, then, can you do on your own to save the situation?

Interestingly, you can ask the customer's help in reaching a solution: "What would you think is a fair way to handle this?" If the client's request is within your authority to grant, do so. If not, counter with an alternative proposal. If the customer still isn't happy, then suggest that he talk to your boss.

What if your customer becomes enraged and threatens you? If the person is standing before you very agitated, with fists clenched, face red, eyes wide open, step away for a moment to ask for assistance. Better to be embarrassed by making a fuss than wind up in a doctor's office. Even a threat from someone on the phone shouldn't be ignored. Notify your boss that one of her clients became emotional and threatened you. She, in turn, should report the incident to your firm's security department in the event the customer decides to visit your office.

Summarizing, customers can become annoyed or irritated for reasons having to do with product or service quality, the way in which they are treated by your firm, or some personal issue or problem they have. When they are upset, and you speak with them, your professionalism in handling the individual's concern can keep the situation from escalating.

10

Defusing Team Conflicts

Some months ago I received an e-mail message from an office professional with her first team leadership assignment. Susan wanted to know how to get her group of office professionals, from various parts of her organization, to cooperate, despite a past history of conflict among the members. She wrote that the tension in the meeting room could be cut with a knife, and that it was making it extremely difficult for her to lead or for the team to accomplish its current mission, which is to identify new applications for the corporate intranet.

She mentioned that the group has had past problems, but they were before her time, and it seems that no one wants to talk about them, which is putting her at a further advantage. She admitted that the emotional climate in the room has caused her to lose her temper, too, on a few occasions. She was feeling particularly frustrated because, she told me, the books she had read on team leadership had made it all sound so simple.

I was able to help her, as you'll discover at the end of this chapter, and I hope I can help you, too, as you assume team leadership, to deal with team conflicts.

The Reality of Leading Teams

Incidentally, Susan isn't the only person who has found a big difference between what is written about team leadership and the reality of leading a team. And with cause. Most business books tend to gloss over such problems as team conflicts, promising that it will be easy for leaders to achieve harmony solely through their leadership position and good communication skills. And it just isn't so.

114

While a new leader's worst fear about conflicts isn't likely to occur—that is, members aren't likely to become so upset that one or more walk out of the meeting room, leaving the leader unsure what she should say or do—conflicts are not unlikely in team situations, given that members probably won't all be in agreement about the group's task or how it is to be done. Unless discussion of the differences is controlled, they can give birth to loud disagreements or unearth previous hard feelings between members.

How to Respond to Team Conflicts

When conflicts arise, as a team leader or member, you have three options:

1. Ignore it. This is likely what Susan's predecessor did. Earlier problems were ignored in the hope that they would go away but, instead, they have remained and festered to the point where members' attention is still on them and not on the team's mission.
2. Confront the disputants in the hope of getting them to recognize how their behavior is interfering with the team's mission. This can work if the leader is supervisor of the team members in conflict. But if the leader has no positional authority over the team, she's more likely to generate a new conflict, with her self-righteous attitude as its base.

   Truth is, when you are leading a team of your own employees, getting tough with misbehaving members is easy because you have your supervisory position to add authority to your critical comments. Because you are their boss, your staff members know that they likely will be appraised based not only on their individual performance but on their participation in the team you lead. You can get that same support even if the members of the team aren't your employees, as long as your write-ups of team member participation can impact member appraisals or team-related rewards. But when you are leading a group of your peers, or individuals whose staff positions make them think they have more clout than the boss's assistant, then your criticisms of others' behavior will generate only hurt feelings or anger toward you.

3. Refocus the group's attention on the operating rules the group agreed to use to achieve its goal and, more important, on the goal itself. Your purpose is "harmonizing," or facilitating discussion, in order to achieve an exchange of different viewpoints without allowing dissension that resembles a dysfunctional family on a "Jerry Springer" show and which can destroy the team spirit so important to achievement of the final mission.

Keep in mind that your intention isn't to get members of the team to agree with one another about everything. Rather, it is to get members to agree enough on the team's goals and the methods they will use to achieve them for the team to move beyond this difference in opinion. Sometimes bringing the conflict into the open reveals that the differences were only superficial; other times, it reveals that the differences were due to misunderstandings; still other times, those in disagreement with the majority may be happy to go on record disagreeing and then agree to overlook their differences in order to achieve the final goal.

After all, there is nothing wrong with conflict within teams. It is when the conflicts get out of hand that problems arise, as in Susan's situation. The key to conflict management in team settings is a three-part formula: (1) well-developed operating ground rules, (2) a clear mission statement or understanding of the team's goal and its importance to the department or organization as a whole, and (3) good verbal skills that allow not only the team leader but members as well to facilitate discussion and manage any differences in opinion that arise—differences with the potential of developing into disagreements and more serious conflicts.

First to the Basics

Teams need self-discipline, and setting operating ground rules can achieve that. The ground rules should take note not only of the work to be done but the team process or group interaction. For instance, if the team will need to work with other groups to accomplish its mission, then the need for that kind of collaboration should be indicated in the ground rules and, if possible, with the means to achieve it.

SAMPLE

Team Ground Rules

1. Members will arrive on time and stay for the full meeting.
2. Meetings will be held every second week, on Tuesdays, during lunch hour.
3. The team will keep to the meeting agenda.
4. Handouts related to team discussion will be distributed two days prior to meetings. Members will come to meetings prepared to discuss the subject of these handouts.
5. The focus of the team will be on its mission; the group will not be distracted by side issues.
6. The team will allow each member the chance to talk and will hear out other members without interruption.
7. Assignments will be made by the group as a whole.
8. The discussions will be kept to the point and professional; the focus will be on issues, not personalities.
9. The team will meet with leaders of other groups once monthly to review their conclusions.
10. All decisions will be reached by consensus. Disagreements will be resolved by multivoting or voting over time, slowly eliminating items until only one workable solution remains.

You may be team leader but that doesn't mean that you set these ground rules. Rather, you work with your team to create the operating guidelines by which the members will operate—and for an obvious reason: You want the group's members to buy into them, particularly rules like #5 through 10, which give you the means to get the team to look beyond a disagreement (either in task or team dynamics) to move forward toward achievement of the team's objective.

To help your team formulate its own ground rules, ask its members to consider what behaviors will detract from the team's mission and what behaviors will contribute to its achievement. Critical to conflict management is raising the question early on: "How will we handle conflicts and disagreements among us?" Input from the team in addressing this issue in the ground rules will support actions you take as leader—and will ensure member support in the event that a difference gets out of hand and two or more team members bring personalities into their disagreement.

Ideally, have the guidelines hang in the room where your team meets, to serve as a reminder to those in attendance of the commitment they have made to the group's management.

Once the guidelines are set, as team leader, you can work with the team to prepare a mission statement or group charter that describes the team's outcome or goal. This is the compelling reason for the team, and it is important that everyone accept the goal and its importance. Remember, in the event of a conflict, it is the means by which you will regain control of the group and move beyond the conflict. Putting a team mission in writing—in a sentence or two—ensures that the members have a clear idea of the project's scope or purpose and, more important, why it is important for members to put aside their differences to achieve it.

Team Mission

To help you write your mission statement, you might want to use a technique called "storyboarding," in which the group begins by calling out a few key words or phrases that describe the team's purpose. As team leader, you then work with the group to get an understanding of what individual members mean by the words or phrases, exploring differences and similarities between the concepts, to come up with a final statement of mission.

If the team is finding it hard to complete its mission statement, you can try a more involved approach to storyboarding, in which members list key words or phrases on sheets of paper before they come to the next meeting. Once members arrive, they tape their sheets to a meeting room wall. Now, as team leader, you go through the sheets, circling words or phrases that seem to appear regularly. On a flip-chart, write these down and then, as a group, work with the team to fashion the final mission statement.

Don't be concerned if finalizing the mission statement takes more than one meeting. You want all the members to be moving in the same direction. You don't want to have to make course corrections. Having the mission in writing also makes it easier to make those corrections should they become necessary.

You should expect some disagreement when you are preparing the mission statement, just as you can expect some disagreements during subsequent meetings. Actually, as you prepare your mission statement, you will get your first insights into how members of the team will work together—and how much conflict management your leadership role will entail.

Facilitating Team Discussion

When managers and team leaders are asked to list a leader's responsibilities, facilitation is usually at the top of the list. As team leader, you are also team facilitator, responsible for a smoothly running discussion, which means occasionally identifying and remedying team behavior that impedes the team's performance.

Following are ten rules for team facilitation. While the tenth and final rule is most pertinent to this book, take a look at all ten rules for good team facilitation, because they all impact conflict one way or another

1. **Ask for feelings or opinions.** For instance, you might ask one team member who disagrees with another's suggestion what they think about the next step, "What brings you to question . . . ?" or "What prompts your suggestion to . . . ?" or "What are some other ways do you all think we can use this information to . . . ?"

    It's amazing how hard feelings can take seed in someone by her not being given the chance to voice her opinion on another's comment, whether she agrees or not. If the situation occurs in a team setting, some members have been known to sabotage the team effort by foot dragging, hoarding of critical information, and the like.

2. **Paraphrase what others are saying.** This technique can help clarify any misunderstandings, including misunderstandings that may prompt angry words about another member's remarks. Just the act of paraphrasing the comment may make the angry team member realize that she is overreacting to the statement of a co-worker. As team leader, you may also want to paraphrase some remark to ensure clarification for the group as a whole: "Let me see if I un-

derstand your position. Are you suggesting that . . . ?" "What I am hearing is . . . . Am I right? "Let me restate the last point you made to see if I understand."

3. **Call on the quieter members for their reactions to comments from more vocal members.** You don't want to put these shyer members on the spot by calling on them by name. On the other hand, they may have insights to add to the discussion. Consequently, rather than ask specific individuals to comment on remarks made, you may want to go around the room for comments from everyone, thereby not putting a spotlight on that more reticent individual. If someone looks uncertain, you can suggest, "Maggi wants more time to think about this. In the meantime, Charlene, what would you say about what we have heard so far?" Later, after Charlene has had her say, you can return to Maggi and ask, "Maggi, what do you think about Charlene's comments?"

4. **Ask for a summary.** Periodically you might want to stop the discussion to review conclusions reached. Not only will this keep your team on course, but it also allows the group as a whole to catch their breath after a heated discussion: "Before we go on, can someone summarize the points we have made?" "I have heard a number of ideas from the group. Would someone summarize what has been agreed upon?" "It is evident that Barbara disagrees with what has been said. Barbara, could you give us three reasons why?"

5. **Ask for more concrete examples.** This moves the discussion from the abstract to specifics, from an exchange of information to specific actions the team can take to move forward. For instance, "Erica, can you give me some examples of what you think we could do?" "Are there other things we should consider?" "Maria, could you add to what Erica has proposed?"

    As you get to specifics, you likely will encounter more differences in opinion. But issues are better resolved early on rather than left fuzzy until late in the project when confusion can lead to conflicts that dead-end the project.

6. **Question whether the group has reached consensus.** Periodically the team may seem to have reached the point where it is ready to make a decision on an issue. At that point, you may want to call

for a vote to see if you are correct that all the discussion is over. "Maria believes Erica's suggestion should be a part of our recommendations. Does everyone agree?"

If the group feels further discussion is needed, then allow that. However, if the group seems as if it can't get over this hump, then you may want to ask, "What do we want the end result to be? What is it we are trying to accomplish here?" Focus the discussion to critical issues.

7. **Call for action.** As leader, you are always moving the team toward completion of its mission. That will demand that you monitor the discussion and, where appropriate, ask, "How do you think we should proceed?" Or, more specifically, "Darlene, how would you suggest we proceed?" Or, looking to the group as a whole, you might comment, "I'd like your suggestions on possible ways we can get started . . . ."

   As suggestions are made, put these on a flip-chart for later discussion. Ideally, wait until all the ideas of the group have been written on the chart before discussing any. Follow a key rule of brainstorming, which is to hold off criticizing any ideas until everyone has had a chance to offer their ideas.

8. **Suggest the next step.** Toward maintaining team momentum, you will have to put an end to conversations and move along to the next item on the agenda or, related to the team project, the next step toward the final mission or objective.

   The closer you get to the end result, the more likely you will encounter differences in opinion—so, the more flexible your agenda should be in order to accommodate time for discussion.

9. **Support a team member.** You may need to make supportive statements to get members of the team to share their feelings: "Grace, you've had your chance to share your opinion. Let's hear from Bibi now." "Let's give Darlene a chance to describe her experience now?" "Jose, you've had your say. Now it's Salan's turn."

10. **Confront disagreements.** How you confront disagreements will depend on the degree of conflict, and the stage of the team's mission in which the conflict arises. But it is imperative that you act imme-

diately when conflict arises. For instance, Helen is sitting quietly in her chair, obviously upset. You might say, "Helen, you seem upset by what you have just heard. Could you share with the rest of us your concerns?"

The majority of the team seems ready to come to a final decision. But there are two members who aren't supporting the final decision. Open disagreements and even hostility are impeding the team from making a decision. Then you need to give those opposed to the proposed actions a chance to have their say. "Sara, Becky, I sense your reluctance to pursue this idea. Do you have reservations?"

Handling Differences

In each instance where you are faced with a disagreement about another's comment or action proposed, give the other party time to think through her argument and respond fully. Be attentive to the person's remarks and don't interrupt. Ask other members of the group for their opinion of what has been said.

Let's say that Sara and Becky have some cause for concern about the actions that the team is planning to take. Rather than either shift 180 degrees to act on Sara's and Becky's ideas, or ignore their doubts and act on the majority opinion, you may want to address the disagreement in a natural manner, suggesting that the group go back and look once again at the problem and the earlier analysis, maybe even engage in some additional brainstorming, to be sure that the issues raised by Sara and Becky have been fully considered.

What if the conflict grows to the point where your worst fear as a team leader—that is, that someone might get angry enough to walk out—is almost realized? What do you do then?

At that point, it is time to stop and acknowledge the existence of a conflict. Even though you might want to get right to the conflict issue, giving the various parties time to cool off is wise. Call a break of 15 minutes or so, during which everyone has a chance to regain composure. You as team leader would also have an opportunity during the break to consider the nature of the conflict and the best way to handle it.

As you consider your dilemma, you need to look beneath the surface of the problem to determine if more than one issue is involved. If you suspect that there is, you will need to address most of these other issues to resolve the conflict. One way to do this is to lead the group in listing and categorizing their concerns. Then ask the group to prioritize the list of issues to determine which one to address first, second, third, and so forth. As you go through this process, keep the group's attention on the team's goal. There may be issues on the flipchart that can be ignored because they aren't critical to accomplishment of the team's given outcome.

Throughout the lifetime of the group, you may encounter conflicts that have only minimal impact on the team's progress. Consequently, any time you encounter a disagreement, it's important for the group to determine if it is central to the team's progress or unimportant and therefore not worth the team's time.

What if some of the conflicts stem from issues of territoriality or turf, or hidden agendas? That is, members may become combatant if they see as threatened some part of their job, an opportunity for advancement, or an idea they have put on the table for team discussion. If the individual's personal objective could threaten the team's achievement of its final result, then it may have to be brought out into the open. If you suspect this is a problem, you may want to go around the room and ask each member, "What are some of your hopes and fears in regard to accomplishing this objective?" It's all right, your members should know, for them to acknowledge their personal goals and desires, even try to meet them through the team, but make clear to all members that the progress of the group has priority over their personal wants, and the latter will not be allowed to keep the group from being as productive as it should be.

Violations of the Rules

Some conflicts arise due to direct violations of the ground rules set at the formation of the team, actions such as:

- Failure to arrive on time, chronic absenteeism, or early, regular departure.

- Lack of preparedness for meetings; work undone on its due date.
- Disinterest in the team's work.
- Frequent and unapologetic interruption of other members when they are speaking.
- Sarcasm or ridicule targeted at another member.
- Refusal to hear out another member; prejudice or narrow- or close-mindedness.
- An assumption of superiority over the other members; efforts at dominating the discussion.

Let's say that a team member disagrees with another's idea and says, "Claire, I never knew just how limited your thinking was until now." You can interrupt the attacker and say, "Leslie, I don't think that's fair. I'd like to hear what Claire has to say." As the attacker looks at you, you can point to the operating ground rules that hang in the room to remind her that she is stepping over the line she herself helped draw.

But sometimes the misbehavior of a member during the discussion can demand more than a reminder about the team's ground rules. Then you may need to take the member aside and discuss her behavior. Once again, since you lack positional power, you may want to refer to the group's ground rules. Alternatively, you can use peer pressure, pointing to how other members of the team will regard the troublemaker's behavior.

Member Responsibilities

Before I get back to Susan's predicament and what I advised, let me remind readers who aren't leading a team yet that they also have responsibilities for defusing team conflict. They include:

- **Keep the end goal in mind.** You can help the team's leader by considering every remark or idea proposed in light of the team's mission and responding with it in mind.
- **Avoid going on the defensive until you are sure you understand a member's response to your remarks.** Listen carefully so you can address the questions raised. You can disagree, but stay calm as you do so. Don't make this into a personal issue.
- **Don't just listen—look for merit in others' remarks.** Even if the remarks contradict yours, be open to what you hear. Even if you

don't totally agree with the opinion, something said may enable you to improve on your idea.

If the group is sold on the other's idea, try to improve on it, addressing any problems you perceive. Don't disagree and simply refuse to accept anyone else's idea but your own.

- **Don't try to out-talk everyone to win over the team.** Let your idea stand on its merit. Don't get emotional or try to wear down the group by hogging discussion time.
- **Don't become antagonistic if someone interrupts you.** We've all done it at some point. If someone does it to you, don't take it personally. Rather, ask politely and calmly, with a smile on your face, for the person to let you finish.
- **Don't become so attached to your own idea that you aren't a good team player.** Sometimes we can get so personally attached to an idea or invest so much of ourselves in it, it is hard for us to accept the fact that others don't see the same merit. How we respond is indicative of our professionalism. We don't take it personally, which means we continue to support the team initiative, working with our co-workers toward a mutually agreeable solution that will satisfy as many of everyone's needs as possible.

Back to Susan

So what did I suggest to Susan? Very much what I suggested here. Susan set ground rules and wrote a mission statement with her team. But she also called her company's training department to arrange for a training program in facilitation skills not only for herself but her team as a whole. She realized that if the rest of the team were skilled in facilitation, they could help her keep the group on course and achieve its goal. Did Susan find out what had been behind the tension among team members to begin with? Actually, no. No one could remember what had happened the year before, and no one cared, and that was fine with Susan. Her group had become a team.

Epilogue

The most efficient way to resolve conflicts is to avoid them. But conflicts are an inevitable part of life. We may be able to minimize the frequency of conflicts, but we can't prevent them entirely. Any time you get two people together, eventually they will disagree. As evidence of that, just consider the story of Adam and Eve, if we discount the contribution of the snake in the Garden of Eden.

If we can't prevent conflicts from ever occurring, we need to be skilled at resolving them—certainly before they cause nonproductive behavior. This is a skill you need to develop regardless of your job title. But, as you move up in your organization, your mastery of the conflict-management skills described here will put you in better stead.

The same advice given here applies to work relationships at much higher levels of an organization, beyond first- and second-management to senior management and the office of the president. Your ability to effectively manage differences is a critical factor in your professional success.

As author I hope that reading this book provides you with insights into why there are conflicts, how our own efforts to ignore conflicts can do more harm than good, how recognizing a conflict can provide the opportunity to clarify issues, and how conflicts can help build relationships and act as motivators for change. But if there is only one message that you get from this book, it is that most differences in opinion don't have to evolve into shouting matches and that most conflicts can be managed.

We read much today about the need for a climate for productive teamwork in our organizations. The collaborative, cooperative workplace is within our reach—if we only learn the knack of managing disagreements constructively. The benefits are not only to an organization's bottom line, benefits resulting from increased productivity and organizational effectiveness. Your ability to manage interpersonal differences also means increased personal as well as professional happiness when you apply the same skills you use in dealing with conflict in the office to your life outside of work.

To begin to practice your new conflict-management skills, go back to the Preface in this book, and read the ten scenarios. Ask yourself, "What would I say or do in that situation?"

Let me go over those scenarios again, and suggest some answers to each.

Scenario #1. Remember, Marge and Jean have different work styles, Marge very structured, Jean very unstructured—actually, disorderly. Jean's disorganization has frustrated Marge so much that she's ready to blow up. In her position, would you let your emotions take control?

It's time for what kids know as a "time-out" for Marge. She may be justified in yelling, but her angry words will only add another kind of difficulty in her relationship with Jean. It is better for Marge to wait until she's calmer, then she could suggest that she and Jean discuss how they might work more effectively together. It may be time to set up some rules about how and where reference books will be kept and how documents will be maintained. How Marge broaches the issue will determine if the meeting is a confrontation or discussion. Marge might want to point to Jean's poor work habits, but she will get further if she suggests to Jean, "You and I have so much to keep track of, we need some systems in place to ensure that we don't mislay important documents or misplace important reference books. Where do you think we should start?"

Of importance, she shouldn't let the problem continue. She and Jean will eventually find themselves playing a version of "The Odd Couple," with her in Felix's role and Jean as Oscar Madison.

Scenario #2. Bryan and Alix disagree with Theresse, leader of their team, about how to pursue their assignment. They also find Theresse to be too dictatorial. In essence, these are work and process problems. If the team has set ground rules at its start, and these ground rules allow for involvement of the entire group in the final decision, then Bryan and Alix have the right to question Theresse's decisions during the meeting if they don't represent the entire group's thinking. They can also discuss Theresse's personal style under these ground rules, although this issue might be handled better after the meeting in a quiet discussion. Alix and Bryan might begin that discussion by telling Theresse, "We were asked by you to participate but today we felt that you were oblivious to our views. We believe others may be feeling this way, too. Can we talk to you about it?"

Note the use of "we" and expression of feelings. There is no finger-pointing: "You" did this or that.

Scenario #3. Mario has been silenced several times during a teleconference by John, who asked him to participate yet seemed not to want him to open his mouth during the conversation. Before Mario complains, he may want to ask himself if John had cause to silence him. Does John know something that Mario doesn't? Would Mario's comments have shifted the flow of conversation in a direction that John didn't want to go or derail it from its current direction? Mario may feel that his time has been wasted and he may be tempted, when next invited by John to participate in a teleconference, to ask sarcastically if he can speak, before accepting the invitation. Instead, he should ask John for his assessment about how the discussion went. During the subsequent conversation, Mario can bring up the points he had wanted to raise during the telephone conversation and check John's reaction. They may have been peripheral to the discussion. Next time, Mario may want to discuss with John their objectives before the telephone conference.

Scenario #4. Erin has said some unkind words to Antonia, your friend, and you may be tempted to go to Antonia's defense. But this is Antonia's problem, not yours. You may go to the ladies room to be sure that your friend is feeling better, you may hear her out, but you shouldn't take sides or encourage further animosity between the two women. If you want to help Antonia, you should encourage her to speak calmly with Erin to resolve the problem developing between them.

Scenario #5. Since Antonia didn't invite Erin to a group lunch when a former employee came to visit, you know that she and Erin are still feuding. Further, the rest of the office professionals are taking sides. As assistant to the head of the division, you see that work isn't getting done as a result of the problem. You could bring the problem to the attention of the division head, since it has become a department problem. But if your boss is very busy, you may want to see, first, what you can do by talking both to Antonia and Erin and volunteering to act as mediator to help them resolve their differences.

Scenario #6. You feel that you were doing more than your job description. When you didn't get back to a salesman with some information, he lost the account, told your boss, and now your boss has you on the carpet. Don't get defensive. Hear Tim out. Even accept responsibility for not following up with the promised information. Then explain why it happened. And move on to discuss how such problems can be prevented in the future.

When the salesman calls later demanding new information immediately, see that he gets it. If he brings up the matter, apologize—and leave it at that.

Scenario #7. You didn't know that Marietta felt as she does—isolated from the rest of the group. Ask yourself if you have unconsciously done so. If you have, an apology is in order. If you haven't, then an explanation about your past friendship with Blair should do. Then go one step further: Ask Marietta how you might make her feel more like a member of the group. And together, go out with Blair to lunch.

Scenario #8. Bill can still get a temp. You did a terrific job prior to the conference, and he promised you that if you did double-duty prior to the meeting, he would give you time off to sightsee while in Vegas. Explain how exhausted you are and how you need time off, as he promised you could have. If it's a matter of cost, offer a compromise. You'll work in the mornings and see that the temp knows what to do, but you want afternoons and evenings off to enjoy yourself. If he refuses your compromise, you will have no choice but to do the work while in Vegas. Do your job well; don't sulk. But consider whether or not this is someone

with whom you want to continue to work. Lack of trust is a real problem—look for a position elsewhere within your organization with
someone you can trust.

Scenario #9. You may want to ask others on the team if they agree
with Margaret that the group should vote on the proposal then get
back to their desks. Look around you. Say, "Margaret, I'm not sure
we're ready to make a decision. Angela, do you feel we have enough information on the table to make a decision? Arthur, do you think the
group is ready to vote on this idea?"

If Margaret continues to be a thorn in the team, you may want to talk
to her about the worth of the team. Ask her, "How could we make the
team more worthwhile?" "What issues should we address as a group to
make the sessions more productive for the group?" Hear her out. Even
the most obnoxious people can have great ideas. And implementing
one or two of Margaret's suggestions not only may improve the work of
the team but also may improve Margaret's disposition.

Scenario #10. When Todd comes to handle a computer problem, he
is unpleasant to the person who called, throwing technobabble to show
his superiority. The next time that he says, "You wouldn't understand"
when you ask him what was wrong, stop him and say, "I think I would
if you would explain the problem. Further, if I know what happened, I
will know how to avoid the problem in the future."

Pause.

So long as you stand in front of him, there is little that Todd can do but
offer to explain the problem to you. Ask questions. If you need to write
some of his instructions down, do so. When he is ready to leave, say,
"Thank you. I will follow your instructions so the problem doesn't
recur. I really appreciate your taking the extra time with me." Like they
say, a little honey can tame the grouchiest of bears.

How did you do? It's not so important that you and I agree on each and
every situation—actually, it's not necessary for us to agree on any—only
that you understand that in each instance you have an opportunity to
either prevent a conflict from arising or defuse one that already exists.

Resolving conflicts demand:

- A willingness to hear out the other party.
- A lack of defensiveness as you listen to the other person's opinion.
- A calm presentation of your own side of the issue.
- A willingness to listen to the other person's response.
- A continuation of this pattern until you've reached a point where your viewpoints are clear to one another; and finally.
- A desire to find a point of agreement or common thinking from which you can reach an accord, even if it's to agree that you can't agree but that you will treat each other with professional respect.

Index